The Organic Curriculum:
Organizing for Learning 7–12

The Organic Curriculum: Organizing for Learning 7–12

Robert Hunter
and
Elinor A. Scheirer

 The Falmer Press

(A member of the Taylor & Francis Group)
London, New York and Philadelphia

UK   The Falmer Press, Falmer House, Barcombe, Lewes,
            East Sussex, BN8 5DL

USA   The Falmer Press, Taylor & Francis Inc., 242 Cherry Street,
            Philadelphia, PA 19106-1906

First published 1988

Library of Congress Cataloging in Publication Data is available on request

ISBN 1 85000 249 5
ISBN 1 85000 250 9 (pbk.)

Jacket design by Caroline Archer

Typeset in 11/13 Bembo by
Alresford Typesetting & Design, Alresford, Hants

Printed in Great Britain by Taylor & Francis (Printers) Ltd, Basingstoke

Contents

Acknowledgements

Our thanks are due to the many people who have influenced and shaped our thinking and practices over many years. In particular, we are grateful to the children and staff of Rosedale Middle School for their inspiration and encouragement.

Preface

What we offer is a way of thinking — about children's learning, about teaching and about how we can make decisions about our teaching for the benefit of children's learning. In the process of sharing our perceptions, we also raise issues which should encourage the professional dialogue necessary for the development of educational thinking.

The Organic Curriculum presents a way of looking at children and of working with them which we believe facilitates their growth in meaningful and multiple directions. This approach can only be understood through careful analysis of and reflection upon teaching practices and their consequences. We have used many teaching–learning examples here in order to make very real what might otherwise be a rather abstract set of principles. Out of these examples we then offer a framework which teachers can use in making decisions about what they do with children. This framework is intended as a guide for teachers as they develop their own best approaches to the challenges of their classrooms.

Our view of what primary education can be is one which is enhanced by several strands of curriculum organization, such as child-centredness and a process-oriented approach to teaching which emphasizes the role of concrete experiences in learning and the integration of content areas. We believe that the mandates which educators are currently receiving speak to the results which society desires for its young and to the expectations and hopes it holds for their learning. The role of the teacher remains that of professionally examining the various options available in terms of learning experiences for children and the teaching styles appropriate for providing them in order to achieve those goals. This is the case, whether or not the individual teacher agrees with the goals which have been identified and wherever the teacher may be serving.

We view the teacher's world as one with powerful financial, cultural, political, historical and organizational constraints which vary from place to place, but also one with many areas open to decision-making. What we intend to provide is a rationale for certain decisions which teachers can apply to their own situations. We offer approaches to working with children which are realistic in the context of the demands being placed upon teachers in the late twentieth century. We hope that our view may encourage an evolutionary attitude toward education as teachers piece together the requirements of society with their professional knowledge and experience.

The Organic Curriculum draws together many themes which have characterized education over the years. As such, it is not a new approach to teaching as we shall point out in Chapter 1. However, the unique mixture of elements and the ways in which these have shown themselves in current practice are at a particular stage of development which demonstrates a maturing of teaching's art and craft hewn carefully over the years. Indeed, it seems entirely appropriate that we should attempt to describe this approach and to outline how it may be implemented.

While *The Organic Curriculum* synthesizes many components of curricular thinking across both teaching and school administration, it is neither inclusive of the many topics discussed in those fields nor exhaustive with regard to any one of them. The deliberate selection of topics demonstrates the integrity of the concept of the organic curriculum and its connections to underlying psychological and sociological generalizations.

We have also implicitly acknowledged that teaching in schools and managing them are complementary tasks, necessarily working together toward a cohesive approach to the education of children. Consequently, we believe that teachers should be aware of what principals and headteachers need to consider and that principals and heads should remind themselves of what teachers confront when implementing curriculum. The organization of this book provides a means for each group to understand the challenges faced by the other within the organic curriculum.

The two of us have come to the organic curriculum by separate routes, one by in-depth experience over many years as a teacher and headteacher and one through qualitative research, study and analysis. Together, our roles provide the complementary perspectives of the practitioner and the theoretician, though each of us admits to both in our individual lives.

We also provide two cultural points of view of the organic curriculum, one English and the other American. While the interplay between the English and American educational systems has been substantial over the last twenty or so years, it is also clear that professional perceptions of what ought to occur in schools do differ. There are substantial differences between English educational practice and American educational practice which can lead to differences in how we view the purposes of schools, the way children grow and learn and how teachers are to respond to the demands placed upon them. Such differences present very different starting points for teachers and for those working with teachers. They also present us with the challenges of comparative education which encourage us to broaden our repertoire of practice from a solid understanding of what others do.

We constantly find ourselves faced with the intriguing paradox of our approaches being so much alike and yet so different. Yet, herein lies a strength. It has forced us to consider very carefully the terminology we use and to explore thoroughly the concepts thus represented. And, it is out of a desire to connect these similarities and to bridge these differences that we have pursued the organic curriculum — as a kind of synthesis of good practice applicable in many settings on both sides of the Atlantic, an approach to teaching not bound exclusively to one culture.

The Organic Curriculum is intended to appeal to several audiences. Pre-service teachers can benefit from its description of an approach to teaching as they develop the background and skills necessary to the evolution of their own teaching styles. Since the book outlines an integrated approach to teaching, it complements those teacher education materials which address the separate domains of teaching. A second audience includes teachers already in the classroom; through consideration of the text, they will be able to develop more fully their styles and to reflect upon what they do with children. In addition, school administrators, headteachers or principals, will find the text helpful in identifying those practices characteristic of teaching in schools which promote interactive learning, the conditions necessary for their development and the approaches which can foster staff growth in appropriate directions. In all cases, we wish to encourage our colleagues to sample the organic curriculum so that its benefits and challenges can be more clearly appreciated.

Therefore, the book primarily describes and analyzes an interactive approach to teaching children between the ages of seven and twelve. It also includes discussion of its theoretical and historical underpinnings, as well as practical suggestions and guidelines for putting such an approach into operation. As such, theory and practice are given a balanced presentation. Work in the various content areas is also presented in order to demonstrate how basic learning processes are developed and how skills are integrated across the content areas. We describe what happens in the organic curriculum without trivializing its complexity through either over-generalization or reduction to formulae. Because the description also encourages analysis and critique, we thereby support the efforts of reflective, intellectual teachers who eagerly assume the responsibilities of professional decision-making.

Finally, throughout the text we have sought the use of nonsexist language. However, the reader will note occasions where individuals are described or referred to as having a particular gender. We have chosen to specify gender in order to personalize the discussion or to reflect the real people who generated the examples we share.

Part I
The Roots of the Organic Curriculum

Chapter 1

Tradition and Evolution

The organic curriculum has roots in the ideas and practices of many educators. This chapter outlines several of the philosophical, conceptual and historical bases which have nurtured its evolution. Such a tracing of its development underscores the continuity of the organic curriculum with a significant stream of educational thought in both the United Kingdom and the United States.

What follows suggests how this approach to primary schooling came into being, both in terms of its theoretical development and the evolution of practice associated with organic teaching. It is not, however, either a history of primary education or a discussion of philosophical schools of thought *per se*. Nor can it be a justification for the existence of the organic curriculum, either in terms of developing an inclusive rationale or formulating a sufficient response to its likely critics. Rather, the purpose of this discussion is to demonstrate the rich origins of the curriculum approach labelled here as 'organic'.

The threads of thought and practice to be described have become interwoven over the years into a coherent way of teaching children aged seven to twelve. Being aware of the interrelationships among these ideas is central to understanding the breadth of influence on the shaping of the organic curriculum and the difficulty faced in explaining its complex character. Yet the more one appreciates these influences, the more likely one might be able to implement it knowledgeably and with conviction.

The Tradition Leading to the Organic Curriculum

The concept of the organic curriculum is not specific to any one culture. A long tradition exists in both England and the United States which supports organic teaching, thus making it yet another step along the way in the growth of teaching practice.

Determining the origins of any phenomenon as complex and as endemic to a modern Western culture as a school curriculum poses an initial problem of limits. One needs to decide how far back into historical accounts to proceed and how inclusive one's perspective should be. In some sense the bases for all of our modern social institutions and their varying practices lie in Renaissance and Enlightenment views of the nature of the person and of the ways of knowing which in turn derive from Greek and Roman philosophy. Then, too, with an institution such as the school woven so tightly into the fabric of society, there is an immense range of developments outside its walls which influence the ways it functions and the reasons for its operating in those ways. Selection, therefore, has governed this analysis, with all of the difficulties inherent in such decision-making. The result is a brief but hopefully measured and representative presentation of the major forces which have influenced the development of the organic curriculum.

The organic curriculum relates to several approaches in primary-level schooling which have emerged over the last seventy years. This is not to ignore the standard list of thinkers who are considered to be influential in the development of ideas basic to conceptions of modern primary education, among them Rousseau, Pestalozzi, Herbart, Froebel and Montessori. Rather, this discussion will offer a broad picture of practice and of the thinking which related to such practice. For example, the 'progressive' education of the 1920s and 1930s, the teaching described and advocated by the Plowden Report (Central Advisory Council for Education [CACE], 1967) and the American 'open classroom' of the 1960s and 1970s are all clearly part of the same tradition from which the organic curriculum arises. Numerous other educational efforts are also members of this tradition.

An early example of progressive education was Marietta Pierce Johnson's Organic School in Alabama founded in the early 1900s (Cremin, 1961). Built upon the ideas of C. Hanford Henderson and G. Stanley Hall and the early writings of John Dewey, the school focused on developing the entire organism, body, mind and emotions. The approach was informal in which children were to grow according to their own abilities and in consort with an inner satisfaction.

John Dewey's later analyses of the child's relationship to curricular arrangements (1902), the demands of schooling in a democracy (1916), the options in organizing knowledge (1931) and the role of experience in education (1938) established a base for many attempts to reconceptualize the nature of primary education. Indeed, Blenkin and Kelly (1987) state that Dewey's work was the 'culmination' (p. 17) of the theories of many in the Enlightenment and Romantic traditions because it meshed child-centred concerns with a social philosophy designed for the twentieth century. Spurred on by the early example of the Laboratory School in Chicago, experiments with 'progressive education' worked to create in the United States what has since been named the 'progressive education movement'.

In many cases, though, these efforts fell prey to the dangers inherent in any movement. Some educators were caught up in the momentum of innovation and adopted the approaches without fully understanding the underlying rationale for them; others faced lack of community under-standing and were unable to explain this view of schooling to them to their satisfaction. Still others failed to adapt approaches to fit particular edu-cational contexts which led to inappropriate and hence unsuccessful practices. The movement itself suffered from several problems, among them distortion of its principles by both advocates and critics and a failure to develop in accordance with changes in society (Cremin, 1961).

In spite of these results, the progressive education experience in the United States left a significant legacy. Cremin (1961) argues that regardless of the success of the progressive education movement, its basic tenets had by the 1950s transformed the nature of American education and had indeed become its conventional wisdom. Doll (1983) also observes that while the essential model of education did not change in response to the progressives, the sense of ideals did shift from associationist views of learning to an acknowledgement of developmentalism. Progressive education modified and humanized the earlier model by softening its effects. His optimistic per-spective embraces the view that further educational change will occur because of the demands of a post-industrial society and that now there is a strong likelihood for a 're-visioning' of progressive education based on a new paradigm derived from the Piagetian model of growth and develop-ment.

If Doll offers us reflection on the American experience with pro-gressive education, Stewart (1979) discusses progressive education in England. Experiments for young children, along with progressive indepen-dent schooling for a minority of the middle class, represented early efforts. The former have evolved into a rich legacy still seen in many state-supported child-centred primary schools.

The Hadow Report of 1931 (cited in Richards, 1984), described by Marriott (1985) as the first official expression of progressive educational ideologies, contributed to the definition of the primary tradition in its rec-ommendation for reorganizing schools into primary and secondary levels. It also supported the integration of subject areas and stressed the importance of concrete experience in learning. While school reorganization was finally accomplished in the 1960s (Blackie, 1967), the other dimensions of Hadow were largely ignored (Razzell, 1968).

During the 1920s, 1930s and 1940s, the shaping of primary teaching practice came about principally through the efforts of individual practitioners working in their professional capacities in schools. The stories of Robin Tanner (1981), Peter Stone (DES, 1949) and Sybil Marshall (1963) and the talks of Christian Schiller (1979) described and reflected upon approaches to teaching which influenced other practitioners over the years and thus contributed to the climate in which the Plowden Report was published in 1967. Along with descriptions of what was good practice, these individuals also provided strong rationales for what they advocated and thus were not atheoretical in their perspectives.

This development of practice was not a movement in the sense that American progressive education became a movement. The writings of the time focused on actual teaching and did so in ways that invited others to consider the approaches but only in light of their particular circumstances. Further, the spread of these approaches occurred quietly over long periods of time and in various parts of England as the result of practitioners influencing subsequent generations of practitioners. The development of the approaches was not always smooth and practice was at times not fully grounded, but a tradition evolved which was carried forward.

Significant public attention to the principles of progressive education occurred again in both England and the United States during the late 1960s. The Plowden Report was initiated approximately thirty years after Hadow to determine 'how far the intentions of Sir Henry Hadow and his committee had been carried out and how well they had stood the test of time' (CACE, 1967, p. 1). As a follow-up to Hadow, it endeavoured to assess whether data on child development were the same as a generation earlier and to relate new perspectives on learning to the conclusions of Hadow. The publication of the report in 1967 gave recognition to practices which many teachers had been developing and following for some time, though the school world Plowden described and advocated was clearly not the reality everywhere. Most interestingly, though, the introduction acknowledged that English primary education had already developed a high reputation worldwide.

Based on survey techniques, the report described a wide range of primary schools throughout England and then formulated an extensive series of recommendations. The recommendations supported the expansion of these practices to all primary schools as part of a well-founded process of reform based upon years of trial and development in pockets of innovation in many different areas of England, notably in the West Riding of Yorkshire, in Oxfordshire, in Leicestershire, in Hertfordshire and in Bristol and London.

Interest in adopting Plowden progressivism grew rapidly. Alexander (1984) notes that 'Plowden was treated as an inspirational document, and one which ostensibly legitimised the progressive aspirations of thousands of teachers' (p. 11). The report seems to have been part of the political mood of the 1960s which placed education in focus because of its likely desirable social and economic consequences (Marriott, 1985).

Following Plowden's publication, descriptions of teaching practices were prevalent as guidelines for others who wished to implement the more informal approaches. Brown and Precious (1968) vividly discussed the nature of the integrated day in both infant and junior schools as a practitioner-oriented 'rallying call'. Marsh (1970) described how the teacher should work 'alongside the child' by stressing the importance of teacher observation and the centrality of children actively working with a wide variety of materials throughout the many areas of the curriculum. Less romantically but with as potent a message, Razzell (1968) outlined the implications of Plowden for teaching in junior schools within both an historical and social context, suggested avenues for the development of practice and warned of the dangers of a popular movement in education.

Other educational leaders in primary schools such as Sir Alec Clegg (1971) and John Blackie (1974) also guided practice by acknowledging historical and philosophical contexts, expressing caution in reference to meaningful change and clarifying the essential characteristics of child-centred approaches. The publication in 1979 of Christian Schiller's thoughts on primary education gave educators further direction. His far-reaching influence over the previous fifty years represents that of one who intuitively knew how to encourage children's learning and could inspire others in the pursuit of their teaching practice. Griffin-Beale (1975) comments that Sir Alec Clegg thought Schiller was the most influential person in the development of modern English primary education. While his purpose was not to offer didactic help to those who sought to teach children in less formal or traditional ways, Schiller's professional example as well as his teaching through metaphor and description supported more than a generation of able practitioners and still stimulate reflection on difficult questions of teaching and learning.

The years after Plowden also saw discussion of the evidence contained in the report. Marriott (1985) echoes the analyses of others in his examination of the data from which the generalizations arose.

> At most, only schools in Categories 1 and 2, 10 per cent of all schools, could be described as having achieved all or most of the Committee's recommendations, with perhaps Category 3, 23 per cent of schools, being well on the way, and another somewhat indeterminate proportion showing some promise. (p. 31)

But the report was, as indicated earlier, influential because of the tone suggested in the text rather than because of the strength of the evidence.

Marriott further describes how subsequent writers who interpreted and extended Plowden implied that massive change was occurring; for example, John Blackie and Sir Alec Clegg used language which created the impression of a revolution in primary education. This self-perception was then reinforced by American writers who observed practices which were assumed to be the norm and extolled their virtues.

Shortly after the publication of the Plowden Report, American interest in the practices of English primary schools was indeed nurtured by the journalistic writings of Featherstone (1971) and Silberman (1970). Educators in the United States were ready to undertake substantial change because of keen social awareness that the educational system was not doing all that it needed to do in order to equalize opportunity for all children and to create a 'great society'. Out of the extensive coverage and discussion of what was happening in British infant schools developed what was termed the 'British Infant School' approach to teaching which later evolved into the 'open classroom' movement in the United States. The movement rapidly gained many advocates and captured the imagination of many educators, even though there was limited specificity about what was being sought.

American publications burgeoned which described what happened in English primary education and in effective open classrooms (for example, Eisner, 1973; Fisher, 1972; Kohl, 1969; Rathbone, 1971; Rogers, 1970; Weber, 1971). The literature also included guidebooks designed to help practitioners implement open education programmes (for example, Morgan *et al.*, 1981; Stephens, 1974). Yet, Silberman (1970) characterized informal practices as 'less an approach or method than a set of shared attitudes and convictions about the nature of childhood, learning, and schooling' (p. 208). There were efforts in teacher education programmes to develop these attitudes, skills and practices (Ishler and Ishler, 1974; Silberman, 1970), but little help was available to those inservice teachers who realized that their settings required careful transitions if substantial and lasting change were to occur. The American educational profession at this time seemed to divide itself into one group romantically attracted to a new way of teaching which promised release from the stifling experiences of a rigid schooling, a second group critiquing the views of the first and a third group struggling to see how to accommodate the needs and interests of the children with traditional concerns for knowledge acquisition and meeting the needs of a complex society.

A bandwagon atmosphere was dominant despite cautions to ground practices in careful thought about underlying philosophical and psychological principles (O'Brien, 1974). Open education developed into an ideology rather than a coherent, well-founded alternative to the prevailing educational realities of the day. Myers and Duke (1977) provided a representative indictment:

It would seem that educators in the United States have collected under the label of open education a number of 'best existing practices' and imbued them with the aura of an ideology. Whilst it is a healthy tendency to seek out such tried and true methods and combine them for optimum effectiveness, it is a mistake to see such a package as substantially different from 'good' education. Open education lacks the army of extraordinary teachers, the knowledge of how changes can be effectively introduced, the broad-based active support of administrators and citizens and the conceptual clarity to make it a realistic alternative for the average school. (p. 227)

Much of the problem lay in the lack of clearly defined constructs delimiting open education to which the profession could agree (Giaconia and Hedges, 1982; Horwitz, 1979; Marshall, H.H., 1981), even though there were some observational studies (for example, Brandt, 1975; Evans, 1975; Resnick, 1972) involving the use of various instruments which suggested characteristics of the more informal teaching approaches.

This state of affairs inevitably led to difficulties in interpreting the inconclusive research results on the effects of open education in the United States. Since programmes were compared with little attention to the ways in which they actually differed, interpreting any differences in outcomes was a confusing task at best. Ellsworth (1979) called for research based on operational definitions of open education and for the further development of instruments designed to discriminate among various approaches to schooling and to assess the degree to which various programmes actually implemented open education.

All of this is not to say that there were no attempts to delineate the nature of open education. As early as 1972, Barth outlined a set of twenty-nine assumptions about children's learning and the nature of knowledge which seem to characterize both the practices and writings of open educators. His correlation of assumptions with both English and American sources underscored the intimate connections between primary teaching practices on both sides of the Atlantic. Thomas and Walberg (1975) performed a content analysis of significant literature on open education in which they defined themes and identified systematic trends. Butt (1977) combined the English and Canadian perspectives when he devised a conceptual system for the open classroom with the intent of thereby facilitating research efforts directed toward determining the effectiveness of open education.

Although the heyday of unabashed American interest in open education has passed, there is still concern for incorporating characteristics of open education into the mainstream curriculum. Noddings and Enright

(1983) analyze the 'promise' of open education by differentiating the practice and movement of open education from open education as a model. They note that many of the influential works on open education restricted themselves to the use of romantic and imprecise language to describe actual examples of successful classrooms. Little attention was given to the open education movement as a manifestation of a more pervasive model. To the end of making explicit the model so that in the future it may emerge in a more coherent fashion, Noddings and Enright discuss five fundamental beliefs of open educators:

1 children interact with their environments and other people, with the recognition that knowledge too is interactive;
2 the learning process itself is continuous, relating to children's previous experiences and present interests and leading to subsequent experiences;
3 the focus of learning is unbounded, with material found in experiences outside the school as well as in the activities and subject matter provided by the teacher;
4 the learning process is social and includes this interaction as both a means and an end to the broad range of educational goals;
5 learning is a transcendent experience, going beyond itself and yet only a part of whatever it means to be fully human.

These beliefs form both the cornerstones of the model of open education and the central legacy of the earlier open education movement.

The mid-1970s saw both sides of the Atlantic reconsider their fascination with the teaching approaches associated with Plowden and open education. Several factors influenced such reevaluation, from the emergence of anti-progressive educational critique (Alexander, 1984) to economic austerity, a decline in the number of primary children and an increase in government control of education (Marriott, 1985). The United States has witnessed the 'back-to-basics' movement growing out of a disillusionment with the research results on open education and the calls for accountability in education. These suggest American concurrence with Marriott's (1985) assessment of the changes in England: that they represent a fundamental movement from progressive ideas towards neo-idealist views of education. However, this brief overview also contends that while movements seem to have come and gone on both sides of the Atlantic, there has been some consistent development of solid theory and practice to support such sporadic efforts.

In the past ten years, the English teaching profession has observed the great rate of publications emanating from the Department of Education and Science. A series of surveys of primary education appeared which described what was occurring in schools and why. The Primary Report (Department of Education and Science [DES], 1978), with its follow-up accounts of schools surveyed by the age-ranges included in them (DES, 1982a; DES, 1983; DES, 1985b), presented results and offered commentary which generally acknowledged the more progressive teaching approaches while also noting the national concerns for achievement in various curriculum content areas.

Teaching in these content areas has over the years been examined in great detail. The Bullock Report (DES, 1975) on language and the Cockcroft Report (DES, 1982b) regarding mathematics focused on their respective subject areas; however, they also underscored the close relationships of those areas to the rest of a well-conceived primary curriculum and stressed the role of first-hand experience in enabling children's learning. Similarly, the framework outlined by *A View of the Curriculum* (DES, 1980) supported both meeting the basic educational needs of all primary children while also maintaining a broad curriculum implemented flexibly and in response to the characteristics of individual children, classes and schools.

Related points could be made in reference to the more recent materials in the 'Curriculum Matters' series. The description of *The Curriculum from 5 to 16* (DES, 1985a) presents an overall view of curriculum concerns and emphases exemplified in the numerous follow-up discussions by subject areas. The primary focus is, to be sure, upon aims and content rather than upon the context within which learning occurs or the processes which are followed. Yet, when examined in relation to each other and accompanied by the responses from the teaching profession and the general public (for example, DES, 1986), their recommendations for direction and for principles of teaching are not necessarily inconsistent with the good practice which has been evolving in primary schools for many years. Likewise, the parent *Better Schools* White Paper (DES, 1985c) set forth policies and a programme of action which, while clearly indicating that central government was unequivocally asserting the need for general agreement on curricular intentions in order to raise standards, still allowed for interpretation and application at the local level. Thus, even though the critiques of many of these publications (Alexander, 1984; Blenkin and Kelly, 1987) do indeed raise fundamental issues about their assumptions and methodology and about their impact on the culture of the school, an optimistic interpretation still acknowledges room for professional decision-making at the juncture of the teacher interacting with the child to forward learning.

Beyond Ideology: The Organic Curriculum

Educational literature in recent years has also focused on understanding more completely what is indeed occurring in primary schools. This would appear to be part of the sociological tradition exemplified earlier by Blyth's (1965) analysis of English primary education and later by Easthope's (1975) examination of various educational theories in relation to evidence drawn from school realities. The latter's focus on open education and the progressive ideology is of particular relevance here because such examination juxtaposes their views of the individual as learner or teacher against information about the actual school experience. These academic considerations raise important questions about the genesis and development of ideological views of schooling which must be addressed if practice is to have a sound foundation.

In a similar vein are Marriott's (1985) comments that empirical evidence has challenged the pervasive belief of progressive practice being widespread in primary schools, an ironic reflection upon the intense debate which arose from Plowden. The large-scale 'ORACLE' project (Observation Research and Classroom Learning Evaluation) conducted by the University of Leicester has provided evidence drawn from observational study of primary and middle schools that:

> the general pattern of the traditional curriculum quite certainly still prevails, and has not changed in any fundamental way, let alone vanished. Such claims appear to have been founded in mythology. . . . One thing that does seem clear is that 'progressive' teaching, if by this is meant teaching having the characteristics defined by the Plowden Report, hardly exists in practice. (Galton, Simon and Croll, 1980, pp. 155–6)

The ORACLE project identified different teaching styles reflecting actual teaching patterns (Galton, Simon and Croll, 1980) and reported the performance of children in basic skills and study skills (Galton and Simon, 1980). The nature of children's performance in the basic skills revealed that there is no one best teaching style for all areas. However, in examining more carefully the approaches of the most successful teachers in the three basic styles, the project found that these teachers interact frequently with children, foster smooth routines, ask open-ended questions, provide regular feedback and encourage children to work on their own in solving problems. This set of results would indicate that particular styles as such may not be the most critical determinants of children's progress in basic skills but rather the use of specific behaviours. If such a conclusion is supported by continued research, it would seem to reinforce the analytic summaries (for example, Good and Brophy, 1984) of research regarding effective teaching in the United States.

Indeed, the ORACLE research, along with other studies (Bennett *et al.*, 1980; Gray and Satterly, 1981), suggests strongly that effective teaching behaviours cannot be correlated easily to either member of dichotomous categories describing teaching such as 'traditional/open-plan', 'formal/informal' or 'traditional/progressive'. What does emerge from ORACLE, however, is the centrality for learning of interaction with children which the teacher promotes through careful analysis, planning and structure of the teaching-learning process (Alexander, 1984). Further, the issues of learning and teaching are far more complex than polemic would suggest; educational research is capable of demystifying what goes on in the classroom without trivializing that complexity.

The significant work of Alexander (1984) and Blenkin and Kelly (1987) offers the profession much insight as it charts its way toward the twenty-first century. Alexander's challenging analysis and critique of primary teaching emphasize the importance of the class-teacher system and the shared assumptions regarding practice. These lead to the peculiar role of the primary teacher in terms of aspiring to develop the 'whole child' and of defining the curriculum in terms which are similarly holistic. There is a pervasive primary ideology embracing child-centredness as its basic principle and leading to a series of false dichotomies implying choices between either the child or the curriculum, between either experiences or content or between learning or teaching. Yet he acknowledges that the rhetoric of primary education does not lead to uniformity in practice, a reality confirmed by research, notably the ORACLE results described earlier. His objective is to provide a comprehensive analysis of primary teaching so that practice can be rooted in careful thought.

With a somewhat different focus but with very similar concerns, Blenkin and Kelly offer a 'rigorously argued base' (p. 2) for a particular view of schooling. They analyze and critique primary education in order to argue the case for education as process, an approach associated with progressivism and the Hadow/Plowden philosophy but also reflecting more recent developments in understanding children's learning and in curriculum design.

There is thus significant indication that curricular thinking in primary education can proceed beyond the ideological stance and false dichotomies decried by Alexander. Such 'demythologizing' of primary education (Richards, 1980) is crucial if the many issues (Richards, 1982) it faces are to be addressed: concerns regarding the range, structure, appropriateness, consistency and continuity of the curriculum, along with questions regarding standards, teacher autonomy and the control of education. New frameworks for curriculum design may be necessary, an arduous task at best, but they are not impossible to create.

Chapter 2 will expand this discussion of educational literature with particular attention to the themes of child-centredness, the role of experience in learning, the integrating of the curriculum and the process approach to learning. It will thereby set the stage for the description of the organic curriculum as an effort to bring together tradition and critique, practice and theory.

Chapter 2

Learning and Teaching

Chapter 1 described the conceptual and historical bases which have shaped the evolution of the organic curriculum. The consideration of the notion of an ideology of primary education at the close of that chapter set the stage for the discussion which follows.

The focus here is principally upon four strands in the educational literature: the conception of child-centredness, the role of experience in learning, the integration of the curriculum and the process approach to learning. An examination of these strands contributes to the conception of the organic curriculum as a viable representation of learning and teaching in the primary school beyond ideology. It is argued that a careful analysis of these themes will enable the development of a responsive, coherent and rigorous curriculum which is true to both its historical antecedents and the current social context. However, it is beyond the scope of this chapter to provide any more than a flavour of the issues surrounding teacher decision-making which suggests what might be termed the new rigour in educational thinking exemplified by the organic curriculum.

At least since the mid-1970s both sides of the Atlantic have seen a growing number of publications which have critiqued many facets of the primary school. While many educators have expressed concern that this genre of work represents a negativism within the profession, such efforts can also have their positive effects. Indeed, the close scrutiny of concepts and the careful exploration of the range of consequences arising from the application of those concepts can remind us how the reflective examination of our world leads not to inertia but to a more enlightened view of what may be possible. At the present moment, the profession has only a partial understanding of how children learn and the nature of the roles teachers might adopt in furthering this learning. The discussion of the literature selected is undertaken with the purpose of both characterizing some of that understanding and suggesting the questions which remain unanswered.

The Conception of Child-Centredness

That certain material is examined in this section and not in one of the others to follow does not imply that this educational literature is easy to categorize. In fact, much of the work this chapter presents relates to more than one strand of the literature at a time. However, for ease of discussion the contributions are considered in relation to the topic which they principally address.

Child-centredness is indeed the fundamental characteristic associated with progressivism and the Hadow/Plowden tradition in primary education. Yet it has been plagued with misinterpretation, misrepresentation and over-statement.

A starting point for an analysis of this construct would be a consideration of the environment of the primary school, particularly the English primary school. Focusing the discussion here acknowledges that the English primary school has served as inspiration, if not as a model, to educators in other countries with regard to teaching practices which place the child in the centre of decision-making. Blenkin and Kelly (1987) assert that the English primary school evolved as a manifestation of the ideas of Rousseau and subsequent progressive thinkers because it has experienced relatively few external constraints on the development of its curriculum when compared to those experienced by the secondary level of education. In addition, it has received the benefits of the application of the work of developmental psychologists throughout the current century because these insights were believed most relevant to the education of young children. The result has been the emergence of a distinctive 'philosophy' of primary education if not a commonality of practice.

A child-centred approach is generally described as one which has the single axiom of 'starting from the child' as the child is now (Dearden, 1976, p. 49). This axiom leads to certain principles which must be recognized in teaching: children have rights as children; children are individuals; children experience the world in particular ways; children grow according to an inner principle which functions best if children can make choices, follow interests, learn by discovery and express ideas. In this context the teacher becomes a keen observer of children who nurtures their development as interests and readiness to learn become apparent. Dearden remarks on the prevalence of 'horticultural language' (p. 54) used by child-centred teachers to describe what they do with children, language with metaphors of plants unfolding in the process of growth. The aims of this approach thus seem to lie not in content acquisition but in developing children's curiosity, ability to learn, self-expression and autonomy.

Entwistle's (1970) classic and thoughtful statement on child-centred education contributes other dimensions to this concept, as well as exploring the nature of the educated child. For him the fundamental assumption of child-centredness is that learning should 'have *meaning* for the child . . . [and] that the learner comes to possess what he knows' (p. 203). This perspective would involve the need for learning by doing and for activities which are relevant both to other, later experiences and to one's own experience thus far.

Unfortunately, the child-centred position in education often becomes merely a statement against the excesses of other forms of education. If taken to extremes, it can be interpreted as requiring a choice between a series of dichotomies: focusing on the child versus focusing on subject areas, starting from the child versus starting from the teacher, providing experiences versus providing a structured education or developing the child versus responding to society. Dewey lamented the effect of thinking in such extremes because it forces one to develop principles negatively rather than from a positive and constructive point of view (1938). Dearden (1976) has echoed similar concerns regarding such 'one-sided simplifications' (p. 59) which overlook the necessity of designing creative approaches to meet the great variety of challenges in teaching. Entwistle (1970) concludes that 'the educational nexus is triadic — that children require authoritative teachers and a curriculum carefully devised for its cultural and disciplinary values' (pp. 210–11). Indeed, it is this middle ground that deserves the attention of theoreticians and practitioners alike.

More recently as mentioned in Chapter 1, Alexander (1984) has carefully examined the implications for primary teaching of the 'false dichotomies' arising from the child-centred ideology. He argues that this position has developed because it has served as a rationale, or rationalization, for the class-teacher system, that is, the organizational pattern of one teacher who is responsible for the learning of a group of children in a wide variety of content areas focusing primarily on the 'basics'. What is necessary in lieu of ideological language and polemic is the careful analysis of the relationship between the teacher and the child, a relationship consisting of transactions, events and experiences which constitute the curriculum.

Child-centredness has also been critiqued from another, rather different standpoint. Sharp and Green (1975) have questioned whether the intent of child-centred progressive primary education to champion the needs and interests of the child does in fact occur in the classroom. Their exploratory study of classroom practices raises several issues about social realities in these particular settings. They suggested that

the radicalism of the 'progressive educator' may well be a modern form of social conservatism, and an effective form of control in both the narrow sense of achieving discipline in the classroom and the wider sense of contributing to the promotion of a static social order generally. (p. viii)

This interpretation arises from the recognition that in spite of its philosophy, the progressive child-centred school still functions within a broader social context which is stratified and hence will further social interests.

Thus, there is a paradox associated with child-centred progressivism: on the one hand it advocates the rights of the individual to self-development and expression, while on the other hand it provides a means to move children into 'soft control areas' (Sharp and Green, 1975, p. 225). It legitimizes a concern for children's social, emotional, aesthetic and physical development in addition to their intellectual development and hence provides more avenues in which they can be scrutinized and sorted. The progressive approach may even provide a more effective means of social control than more traditional approaches. While Sharp and Green do acknowledge the limitations within which teachers function, they also assert that teachers must use their understanding and consider ways to alter their situations; it is not enough merely to say that individual children are important if children are to be helped to develop fully.

Darling (1986) offers a similar analysis of child-centred schooling. He considers the effects of progressivism when seen as an approach valuing the fundamental nature of the child explained in terms of developmental psychology. Thus characterized, the inherent conservatism of progressive primary education becomes apparent. Existing interpretations of child development may describe what actually does occur, but they do not consider what ought to occur. Further, organizing the curriculum around the needs and interests of children leads to a conservative stance since these do not exist in isolation from social determination, a point Dearden also notes. Therefore, intervention by the teacher is necessary in order to bring about a more equal society; the natural course of development left alone or merely encouraged by the teacher is not enough.

Such critique, however, should not imply that developmental psychology has nothing to offer child-centred progressive education. Blyth (1965) has noted how the developmental tradition provided an alternative approach to schooling which acknowledged the child much more than did earlier forms which stressed exclusively utilitarian basic skills on the one hand and primarily preparation for later education on the other. Doll (1983) even argues that the model of growth and development articulated principally by Piaget presents a new paradigm for our time which can contribute to a 're-visioning of [earlier] progressive education'. Its conclusions based on close observations of children learning can both heighten our understanding of how to structure the learning environment and provide a framework for interpreting the behaviour of children when confronting certain tasks.

Piaget's four stages of cognitive growth and the roles of assimilation and accommodation in learning are indeed powerful tools in explaining how children function in the classroom. They organize and sequence the commonly observed patterns of intellectual functioning in children across various age ranges. They thus clearly inform pedagogical decision-making, particularly in mathematics and science (Alexander, 1984). As a result, firsthand experience remains a requirement in children's learning activities through the concrete operational stage of development; the intellectual demands placed on children will vary according to the developmental level they are perceived to have attained; and differences in children's functioning at a particular time will be interpreted as differences in the rates of development rather than differences in potential. Piaget's perspective therefore provides support for both child-centred and experientially-based primary education.

Such guidelines have proved useful to many teachers even though critiques of Piagetian theory raise questions about both its validity and how it has been applied to primary teaching. Alexander (1984) summarizes the reservations which have been expressed about the research procedures used and suggests the dangers inherent in an overreliance on developmentalism so conceptualized. There is a tendency to underrate what children may be able to do in certain intellectual areas, especially if they are working in environments different from those used in the research setting. Further, the general framework of cognitive development, if followed too closely, may cloud our perception of individual differences and hence of possibilities in individual attainment.

Other perspectives are emerging which can complement the developmental approaches to understanding children's behaviour. Pollard (1985), for example, builds upon phenomenology and ethnography in his study of primary classrooms in order to generate grounded theory. He stresses particularly the importance of high quality relationships among teachers and children in creating the environment essential for effective learning. Acknowledging that both teachers and children are concerned with maintaining their own identities and dignity, he describes the negotiation which occurs as they structure their social order. A positive cycle of teaching and learning emerges when children perceive that fairness exists both in terms of the working consensus of the classroom and with regard to the nature of the tasks set forth. It is then that they become interested and challenged, leading subsequently to enjoyment and learning. The teacher too obtains satisfaction in the process which in turn pushes the cycle to ever higher levels of learning experiences. Pollard's analysis thus clarifies what is meant by those good relationships with children which the developmental view and the child-centred belief system so strongly endorse.

In the context of presenting other studies which also broaden our perspectives on children, Pollard (1987) underscores the necessity of balancing developmentalism with alternative views which acknowledge the role of the social setting and the importance of social interaction in learning. Such work both expands expectations regarding children's capabilities and sensitizes us to the factors which children and teachers consider influential in their lives and the ways they go about making sense of their experience.

Themes such as children's choice and control over their learning become important, along with the influence of social class, gender and race upon the nature of their experience. The complexity of the culture of the school is a central message of this work, with vast implications for the responsibilities of teachers with regard to developing social awareness. Such a sociological stance clearly recognizes the limitations of child-centredness conceived merely as honouring the 'natural' growth of the individual. Reflective teachers will need to respond creatively to the many demands they face in day-to-day classroom life; in so doing, they will likely manifest the essence of child-centredness built upon strong philosophical, psychological and sociological foundations.

The Experiential Strand

The incorporation of the developmental tradition into primary education also acknowledges the role experience can play in learning. In Piaget's theory experience becomes, in a sense, the foundation upon which children learn. Blyth (1984) explores the interaction of experience and development in the course of learning and defines curriculum as the planned intervention in this interaction.

As with child-centredness, the notion of experience in education is more complex than one would initially assume. Entwistle (1970) identifies the basic element of 'doing' as part of learning if such learning is to have personal meaning for the child; further, any activity selected must have relevance to other experiences in other contexts, as well as to the particular situation of the child at the moment. The involvement in first-hand experience also extends to one's developing skill in handling materials and tools. In Hawkin's (1973) terms, the child and the teacher work with materials in a triangular relationship which promotes rich and complex experience so as to further learning.

While Chapter 3 will consider in more detail Dewey's thoughts on the subject, it is necessary to emphasize here that the concept of experience as such for him was insufficient; reflection on experience was also required if the latter were to be educative (Dewey, 1938). Moreover, Dewey used the scientific method of inquiry as the basis for investigation into experience and for reflection on it (Adams and Reynolds, 1981). To these characteristics of experiential education one could add its emphasis on the individual learner who strives for holistic and analytic understanding while using problems or themes which in turn organize study around both process and product goals (Joplin, 1981).

The most common manifestation of experiential learning in practice is the use of topics or projects. Kilpatrick (1918) is usually first associated with the 'project method', which he described as focusing on a 'purposeful act' able both to prepare for life and to constitute current worthy experience for the individual. Over the years the profession has interpreted this approach with varying degrees of success and, at times, simplistically. The relation of project work to the disciplines of knowledge in the curriculum has been problematic, as have been the kinds of activity to be encouraged. There are also considerable questions regarding why many teachers use project work and how the results of their efforts can be assessed (Leith, 1981).

Bonnett (1986) stresses that while structure is important, it is the kind of structure which needs clarification. Skills, concepts and generalizations can provide the necessary structure for that genuine inquiry involving responsibility, risk-taking, learning from error, perseverance, ingenuity and self-evaluation. The most helpful sources for project work are real problems in the social environment or the needs and concerns of the children as they perceive them. Webb (1986) notes that the structure must also allow for progression, for balance among the various areas of the curriculum and for integration among subject areas; in addition, children should share in the creation of the structure so that they may be able to take full advantage of the experience. Conner (1986) stresses that structure in project work must acknowledge the various learning styles of children by providing choices, must permit children to have some significant control over their learning and must provide appropriate matching between the level of work required of children and that of which they are capable. Thus, project work individualizes and so promotes the attainment of its general goals.

The Schools Council description of primary practice (1983) offers several useful approaches to planning project or topic work so that continuity and progression in learning are promoted and children's experiences individualized. Another Schools Council effort focused directly on topic or thematic work; its purposes included helping teachers to carry out such work more effectively in terms of promoting children's thinking and helping them to assess children's progress (Bradley, 1983; Clough, Bailey, Bowley and Coldron, 1985; Eggleston, 1984; Kerry, 1983, 1984a, 1984b;

Miles, 1984). The recommendations resulting from this effort have thus aided teachers in overcoming the weaknesses identified in project work.

Experience and learning also come together powerfully in the realm of classroom relationships. If the teacher is to introduce children to the norms of rational inquiry and investigation, then the teacher must demonstrate respect for those norms in all classroom transactions (Brennan, 1985). Indeed,

> on both liberal and rational conceptions teaching is not an authoritarian exercise of power, nor a patronizing donation of enlightenment. Rather, it is best thought of on the model of sharing, whereby the teacher's own commitment to rationality is shared with the pupils who in the end will be participants with the teacher in one form of life: the life of self-conscious rational beings. . . . [This] sharing . . . involves genuine dialogue between teacher and pupil. (Brennan, 1985, p. 296)

Such concerns for respect, sharing and dialogue become even more critical when the purpose of the teacher is to help children develop those behaviours which are deemed acceptable by the institution of the school. Further, if children are to learn to 'cooperate' in creating a positive classroom climate (Cangelosi, 1988), they must both be shown the behaviours and be given an opportunity to consider their responsibilities and the consequences of the various courses of action which they might follow (Glasser, 1986). The experiential strand in learning thus takes on multiple meanings.

The Nature of Curriculum Integration

This section begins with the recognition that the relationship between various conceptions of knowledge and the ways to integrate their concomitant curriculum areas is necessarily problematic. However, while there is much debate on the issue, several points do emerge.

As with child-centredness, misconceptions influence the discussion (Alexander, 1984). Here facts become identified with all knowledge, curriculum content is confused with pedagogy and choices are forced between concern for the child's activity and experience and concern for knowledge. Alexander's analysis, however, indicates that careful examination of these pairs permits a synthesis which may guide practice. Thus, one can view knowledge as including a variety of forms, one can appreciate that teaching methods inappropriate for children may be replaced by more fitting techniques and experiences can become the avenue through which knowledge may be attained.

Proposals for integrating the curriculum are equally subject to criticism.

If integration becomes a code word for avoiding a rigorous examination of the content appropriate for children to confront, then integration has very little to support its case. More helpful is a consideration of the forms of knowledge and of the ways they might be taught effectively to children. For example, there is the distinction between 'knowing how' and 'knowing that' which Pring (1976) offers. The various lists of rather more expected subject areas (Barnes, 1982) and the classifications of areas in children's development (Alexander, 1984) provide still other possibilities for the identification of knowledge forms and for the organization of what is to be learned.

Integration is proposed for several reasons. It may be a means for the personal structuring of knowledge as opposed to the acceptance of social structures of knowledge (Easthope, 1975). Integration of knowledge may be a more accurate reflection of reality and of our way of understanding it; it may provide a means for approaching practical decisions or for following curiosity which by nature demands the insights from several disciplines of thought; or it may permit the study of complex concepts contained in several different disciplines (Pring, 1970).

Any consideration of integration must remember that subject boundaries do not in themselves hinder all learning; moreover, they are not arbitrary as Dearden (1976) points out. He suggests that one might think of the curriculum as developing in the child a variety of distinct under-standings. They each have different conceptual bases and use different criteria to validate their claims. In Schwab's (1962) terms, they have different aims and use different operations to determine that which is warranted within their ways of thinking. Similarly, Phenix (1964) proposes six 'realms of meaning' which are different in terms of their main ideas, methods and characteristic structures but which together impart a unity. Each area is better understood when it is related to the others, with one of the areas, synoptics, referring to meanings that are in themselves integrative. Therefore, one can see that knowledge may be variously differentiated, but that linkages are also possible across the areas so created.

Dearden argues that because of their power in illuminating human existence, these understandings are central to what is called a general educa-tion. Integrating the curriculum may even impede the attainment of these understandings, though there may be benefit in integrating part of the curriculum for purposes of motivation. This could be accomplished by providing integrated learning experiences for primary children even though the aims may remain subject-specific.

Expanding on these points leads to the possibility of integration as a way to apply what has been learned in more differentiated settings. Integra-tion may also occur in the form of contexts organized by teachers to help children connect their own experiences with academic knowledge (White, 1986); this latter approach stresses the role of teachers and children as problem-solvers and critical thinkers. In essence, integration could become a matter of pedagogy rather than a theory of knowledge.

Alexander (1984) notes that certain curriculum projects acknowledge both propositional and procedural knowledge and modes of inquiry. These projects thus demonstrate the feasibility of organizing and extending children's learning. 'Man: A Course of Study' (MACOS) integrates the curriculum through its focus on concepts and generalizations which extend into several content areas; it also overcomes the narrow developmentalism which assumes that children at a certain stage cannot understand abstractions. Thus is put into practice Bruner's (1960) maxim that 'any subject can be taught effectively in some intellectually honest form to any child at any stage of development' (p. 33). Further, such a focus on organizing principles within rich and varied content areas suggests the role which processes might play in the learning of primary children.

The Role of Processes in Learning

Using processes as a way to structure learning synthesizes the several strands of educational literature presented thus far. Because a process orientation values the distinctions among kinds of human activity, it can be connected to the theme of child-centredness with the latter's concern for growth and individuality. Clearly, processes include within them the notion of experience being central in learning. In addition, processes can serve as a way to integrate curriculum areas without compromising the latter's integrity because they tap into the structures and modes of inquiry which curriculum areas may share.

There are various conceptions of the nature of a process orientation for the curriculum. Blyth (1984) views the primary curriculum as a totality and sees the process approach as central. This 'enabling curriculum' focuses on experience interacting in a balanced way with developmental processes for growth in desired directions.

Blenkin and Kelly (1987) describe their approach as an alternative to curriculum models based on content or on objectives. This progressive model values experience and conceptualizes education as a series of processes of development. They note that the Hadow Report of 1931 supported such a perspective in its concern to 'develop in a child the fundamental human powers' (cited in Blenkin and Kelly, 1987, p. 33). The process curriculum does not negate subject areas, but it does adopt a tentative view of knowledge and claims that organization should be natural and should make sense to children as they organize their own knowledge. The teacher's expertise lies in the ability to help children develop through exposure to knowledge rather than in subject-matter mastery *per se*.

Similarly, Barth (1972) views knowledge as a vehicle for developing thinking processes such as logic, intuition, analysis and hypothesis formation. Entwistle (1970) offers yet another view of processes in the curriculum, that of problem-solving; the problems confronted include not only those which are self-selected but also those posed by the teacher as a means to foster children's learning.

There are numerous lists of processes available which identify what areas a process approach to learning might emphasize. Examples include Berman's (1968) eight, broadly-applicable process skills of perceiving, communicating, loving, knowing, decision-making, patterning, creating and valuing. The field of science lists an array of process skills at several levels, all designed to generate content and through which concepts may be formed (Funk, Fiel, Okey, Jaus and Sprague, 1985). These include the basic skills of observing, communicating, inferring, measuring, classifying and predicting, along with integrated process skills such as identifying variables, constructing graphs, analyzing investigations and so on. It is also possible that more sophisticated conceptions of process may emerge as researchers continue to investigate more fully the nature of children's understandings in the various subject areas.

Dearden's (1976) analysis of the concepts of learning how to learn and learning by discovery provides insight into the nature of processes which the primary classroom purportedly stresses. He suggests that learning how to learn is not as clear a notion as one might think, thus requiring that one consider it not a unitary skill but a family of skills which have wide application. Learning by discovery, as well, has its limits for it may be most useful in mathematics, science and social studies where the material investigated lends itself to either conceptual or actual manipulation and is not as subject to convention as in other areas. The danger is that such effort may become superficial or that insights are sought which are not easily discoverable. Discoveries must be genuine discoveries if they are to promote learning. While there may be the benefits of better retention of knowledge and the acquisition of heuristic strategies, the merits of learning by discovery come in its usefulness for attaining certain kinds of objectives.

Eisner (1982) has also examined in detail issues related to the notion of process. He advocates a broader view of the nature of understanding and of modes for representing it in order to promote cognitive development. In this perspective, then, the teacher can aid the growth of the learner by fostering representation in various forms. Such a stance with regard to learning presents the profession with a significant challenge.

Rowland's (1984) research on the learning processes of children also broadens our understanding of how they develop cognitively. His observational analyses of their overt behaviours in order to ascertain their underlying thinking reveal that learning is an active process in which children reconstruct knowledge from their own perspectives and over which they desire to gain control. The teacher in this conception of the processes of learning acts as a reflective agent who both provides feedback and offers direction.

These accounts would indicate that the concept of a process orientation in the curriculum is indeed powerful. It can complement the developmental, child-centred perspective and can broaden the notion of the role of experience in education. Further, it can offer a means whereby the curriculum may be appropriately integrated. As such, it can inform practice in significant ways.

A brief description of Alfred North Whitehead's (1929) *Rhythm of Education* closes this overview of the literature relating to the organic curriculum. His view of the cyclical process of education reflects the several strands in the literature just discussed and ties them together quite effectively. Whitehead presents a three-stage cyclical process of learning which begins with the stage of romance. Here the learner explores the context of what is to be learned. There is a profound excitement in the mind which supports the move into the stage of precision. The second stage represents a concern for knowledge and for exactness in thinking, for rigorous attention to analysis and detail. However, the learner's efforts at this stage could not have meaning if it were not for the first stage of romance. The final stage is that of generalization. It returns to the experience of romance but with the perspective gleaned from experience during the stage of precision.

The process is cyclical because the stage of generalization will flow into the stage of romance of the next cycle. What has been learned will also inspire the desire to continue learning. One can view the rhythm of education at several levels. In the course of a given period of time, one can discern these cycles. Or, over a lifetime one can appreciate how the stages have come and gone.

Whitehead's view of the process of education seems to resolve some of the issues raised by the literature. The dichotomies associated with much discussion of primary education are notably absent, and balance is restored. The child is honoured while the disciplines of knowledge are met seriously. Experience and engagement around integrated interests are complemented by careful study reflecting subject area values. Relevance and meaning are achieved in the context of knowledge acquisition. Learning is conceptualized as both rigorous and stimulating.

Shaping the Organic Curriculum

There is great risk in attempting to summarize the various forces which have influenced the development of the organic curriculum. Since it is a dynamic enterprise, constantly being created as teachers foster children's learning and reflect on practice, such a summary may contradict its very nature. However, an explication of its principal attributes may serve as an outline or skeleton upon which educators may place their own interpretations and applications as they interact with children and make decisions regarding professional practice. Thus, rather than defining the organic curriculum, what follows will suggest the character that approach will likely take in the primary classroom.

Firstly, some initial points will provide a framework for this discussion. Fundamental to any examination of organic characteristics is the recognition that the teacher is at the centre of the curricular decision-making process. Alexander (1984) asserts that such a position does not challenge the child-centredness of the primary school:

> the concern with the teacher arises because it is the teacher more than anyone else who defines the child in child-centred (or in any other approach), who defines children's attributes, states what their needs are, predicts their potential and evaluates their achievement. It could be argued, then, that knowing oneself as a teacher is one of the basic prerequisites for true child-centredness. (p. 2)

By extension, the organic curriculum requires that the teacher assume responsibility for decision-making and adopt a reflective attitude toward practice.

Secondly, the quality of the teacher's decision-making also includes a clear intentionality about what is to occur in practice and why, with a constant attention to the detail required by such a rigorous process. Without this intentionality curricular aimlessness will result (Pratt, 1987), a condition serving no one's interests.

A third point focuses on the language one uses to describe phenomena. Much of one's value position regarding phenomena comes through in the words chosen for description. For example, Alexander's (1984) analysis of the language of child-centredness reveals its verbal manifestation of an ideology 'inducing a warm, consensual solidarity' (p. 15); such language also establishes false dichotomies between teaching and learning and between the child and society and often uses misrepresentation and caricature. The lessons gleaned from his critique have influenced the description which follows.

Labelling a curriculum 'organic' conjures up several images which on the surface may be pleasant but which may not contribute to deeper understanding. 'Organic' terminology abounds in the literature on child-centredness and on integration of subject areas in primary education. This is friendly, reassuring talk which encourages one to consider such an approach as 'right and proper'. The notion of the teacher as a 'gardener' helping children to 'unfold' may be suggestive or even inspirational, but it is only that: what is necessary is the direction for practice won from the process of challenging and difficult analysis. Therefore, our charge as educators is to explicate from analysis without manipulating unexamined emotions and while avoiding the dangers of reification.

However, an analogy of the 'organic curriculum' drawn in reference to the growth of a living organism may be quite useful if not taken too far. Clearly this approach to teaching is dynamic, both idiosyncratic in particular settings while sharing qualities in common and thus partially illuminated by the concept of growth. Doll (1983) adds to this notion when he reminds us that the roles probability and chance play in human evolution also direct the development of our conceptions of curriculum and teaching practice.

In addition, connection to and interaction with the environment are crucial for a curriculum to be viable; the difficulties Americans experienced when adopting, piecemeal and with little study, English primary-school practices in the early 1970s demonstrate the importance of context. The lesson learned has been reinforced by sociological and political critique emphasizing the intimate relationships between schools and the cultures they serve. As the growing organism behaves in a synergistic way with the other forces upon which it depends, so too are school curricula defined in part by the support they receive and the many contexts in which they lay.

Thirdly, as with a living organism, there is a 'wholeness' or integrity to the organic approach to teaching even while it is conceived of as flexible, fluid, idiosyncratic and evolving. It can neither be reduced to sets of practices to be replicated individually as one may desire at the moment nor be summarized merely as 'a way of thinking' about children, learning and teaching. Stressing its integrity is not to say that the approach is a rigid system, but rather that there are certain defining characteristics which are interrelated and therefore all essential if teaching is to be described as 'organic'.

Chapter 2 has presented a discussion of four principal characteristics which contribute to the integrity of this conception of the primary curriculum: child-centred, experientially based, integrating subject areas and process-oriented. Several other attributes may be useful in clarifying the concept.

The organic curriculum adopts a philosophical pragmatism. Even though such an admission may raise critical issues, its evolutionary nature and its openness to possibilities as yet unknown imply such an orientation. Indeed, the concept of evolution, as applied to all kinds of knowledge including curricular conceptions, is a key theme in Dewey's pragmatism (Kelly, 1986). Curriculum therefore develops much like living organisms.

This is not to suggest, however, that there is no rigour in the decision-making encompassed in the notion of the evolution of teaching practice. Instead, it must be stressed that such decision-making occurs according to certain principles which also recognize the contextual base for what we do in schools. The road followed in such teaching is difficult, but it is also profoundly engaging since one's perspective and insight might evolve as well.

Examples of organic teaching suggest other attributes. O'Brien's (1974) analytic descriptions of practice reflect qualities which are applicable here: there is an aspect of action on the part of both children and teachers; there is concern for the history of children's experiences, as well as for their current activities; there is recognition of the individuality and diversity in learning and in teaching, as well as an appreciation of the connectedness among all participants; and there is the capability of sustaining one's own learning processes demonstrated by children and teachers alike.

Obviously one may also systematically examine the recommendations of the many official reports on primary education, from Hadow to Plowden and thence to those in England during the 1970s and 1980s, for indications of what might be considered congruent with organic teaching practice. Recommendations for practice offered in the literature responding to such reports provide a similar source of useful characteristics. However, these materials relate to the roots of the organic curriculum and, while supportive, do not directly speak to what is deemed exemplary at this point in its evolution. While the organic curriculum is indeed inextricably tied to these antecedents, it is also unique in that it represents both theory and practice as they have developed to this point in time.

Extrapolating characteristics from examples of teaching practice or from recommendations in turn derived from practice has further limitations. The point stressed by Noddings and Enright (1983) and discussed in Chapter 1 bears repeating here: there is a difference between characteristics of an approach to teaching derived from practice and those which arise from a model of an approach. While the former may be more immediately explicit, since they are often stated in the form of examples, the latter have a power which can direct practice over time and across circumstances. At the same time these latter characteristics would not limit the further development of either the model or practice indicated by the model. They also reflect the result of rigorous reflection, analysis and critique which occur when models are constructed. Chapter 3 will describe the key 'elements' of the organic curriculum in an effort to delineate what a model of such an approach to schooling should include.

The Elements of the Organic Curriculum

The organic curriculum designed for seven to twelve-year-olds is a child-centred, process-oriented approach to teaching which emphasizes the role of concrete experience in learning and the integration of content areas. The purpose of this chapter is to outline in general terms what such an approach means when it is put into practice and how these characteristics interrelate.

One may label these four principal characteristics — child-centred, experience-based, integrated, process-oriented — as the key elements in the organic curriculum. The discussion will examine each of these elements separately before considering directly the interrelationships among them when they are combined in teaching situations. This somewhat artificial treatment will make each element clearer so that the subsequent description of their interrelationships might be better understood. However, because each element tends to occur in classrooms along with the other elements, interrelationships among them should also become apparent as the examinations of each element are presented in sequence.

A Child-Centred Approach to Teaching

Perhaps the most abstract of the elements of the organic curriculum is the adoption of a child-centred approach to teaching. Few teachers would deny the importance of considering the child when making decisions about what happens in schools. Yet, transferring that concern into specific patterns of professional behaviour is quite difficult. Indeed, teachers often acclaim that a child-centred approach is easier to identify when it already exists than to describe in general terms so that it can be brought into existence.

While this may be an accurate way to express the very fundamental nature of placing children at the centre of teaching, it still begs the question of what a child-centred approach actually means. As a working definition, a child-centred approach means concentrating as a starting point on issues of children learning rather than teachers teaching. It also means attempting to examine school activities from the point of view of the child rather than from the point of view of the adults in the school. These statements represent the adoption of a particular perspective by teachers when approaching decisions about their teaching.

Phenomenological psychology reminds us of the importance of perception when attempting to view the world as others view it. To a great extent, teachers must attempt to become aware of the influence of their own needs and biases on how they see events. They then may be less likely to incorporate these needs and biases automatically in the view of events held by others. In the context of the classroom, they thus will more likely be child-centred in their decision-making process and less likely concerned with their own wishes.

In the classroom this may simply mean that a teacher supports a child's interest in carefully observing and painting puffins even though many other children in the group have already chosen to do likewise and the teacher may have preferred some diversity in the work. The teacher in this case thereby cedes to the child because the child's selection means something to him/her and will promote his/her learning; and the teacher realizes that the concern for diversity may not be as necessary as originally thought and later discussion of the children's work can accommodate the fact that many of them began with the same subject.

The Piagetian view of cognitive development also becomes useful when attempting to define a child-centred approach to teaching. If teachers adopt a stage view of cognitive development, the learning activities they design for children must be congruent with the way children think and with what experiences they may require at a particular time. This need forces teachers to recognize actively the characteristics of children's thinking which may be quite different from their own. This approach would mean that a teacher's need for efficiency in instruction, often represented by teacher lectures and paper-and-pencil activities, would give way to children's need for concrete experiences and hands-on activities. Thus, the teacher would actively recognize that children require certain approaches to learning which the teacher no longer requires and would support their cognitive view of the world. Such a response is a clear manifestation of a child-centred approach to teaching.

A child-centred approach to teaching thus includes the adoption of guidelines from phenomenological psychology while making instructional decisions and the recognition of principles drawn from Piagetian views in developmental psychology when deciding what and how to teach. Yet, it also includes an informal but fundamental adherence to considering first and foremost how children view their lives at school when designing specific learning activities. This procedure could mean that teachers informally remind themselves of children's point of view by responding to a series of questions such as:

1 What needs of children — cognitive, emotional, social — does a particular planned activity meet? Are the children aware of their own needs? If not, how can they become aware of them?
2 How does a particular activity meet with the children's expectations for the classroom?
3 How can the children feel involved in making some of the decisions about what occurs in the classroom?
4 How can children's interests be incorporated into ongoing classroom activities?
5 What meaning will the children make of the learning activities offered?

Teachers can, in a sense, assess their plans for the classroom against their responses to these questions so as to establish that children are indeed at the centre of the decision-making process. They would, then, determine that work for eight-year-olds which grows out of a visit to a local farm is child-centred; it does meet children's various needs and interests, it matches what children expect in the classroom in terms of the format of activities, it is broad enough and rich enough to allow for children's involvement in directing the emphases of their efforts and it provides a forum in which children can reflect on aspects of everyday living.

Thus far, the discussion here suggests how a teacher might assure a child-centred approach in the classroom when planning for what activities might occur. Placing the child at the centre, however, takes on additional meaning during actual teaching. While no one any longer mistakenly assumes that a child-centred approach to teaching translates into permitting the children to do whatever they wish, the teaching-learning interaction in the classroom still needs careful explanation if it is to be focused on the child.

A child-centred approach requires that the teacher constantly direct attention to children's activity, to observing and analyzing what that activity represents of the underlying thinking processes. The teacher then must provide specific feedback to the individuals so that the thinking processes can be encouraged to become more sharp. The teacher will, for instance, ask children investigating the distance toy cars of different sizes and shapes travel down and beyond an inclined plane what information they are recording and what and how they are organizing it; if children are omitting important steps, the teacher pushes their thinking through posing more questions which will encourage them to identify what is missing. The teacher-child interaction thus begins with the behaviours of children from which the teacher behaviours take their cue. The teacher's behaviours, therefore, are only important insofar as they relate to learning and are not ends in themselves; all that a teacher does is in reference to promoting children's learning.

Children also take an active role themselves during actual instruction to assure a child-centred approach to teaching. They often set their own goals for learning within the framework established by the teacher and with the materials provided by the teacher. Broadly speaking, these self-set goals are influenced by the teacher through the limits established, but they also allow the children to determine some of what they learn and how they learn it. And, because children are most likely to set for themselves activities they can accomplish, their role here assures that principles of cognitive development are recognized and that learning experiences are positive. Therefore, when a teacher requires that children sharpen through painting their observations of what they have experienced, the children are able to approach the task at a level which permits them to succeed; they use techniques of which they are confident, select specific subjects about which they have some knowledge and extend their abilities as the teacher encourages them to build carefully on their solid foundations.

The child is also central in teaching when the teacher attempts to reflect on the quality of what has occurred in the classroom. To be sure, the teacher carefully examines evidence regarding what the individual child has learned which is juxtaposed against what was intended for that child. While such a focus seems obvious, it can sometimes be lost when computing class averages or when accounting for one's professional behaviours to those in authority.

To balance this outsider's view of what the child has learned, a child-centred approach to teaching must also invite the child to reflect on what has been learned. After carefully painting a railway engine observed during a visit to a railway station, a child is asked to describe what part was difficult to represent and why, what techniques she used for the first time or what she thought about the engine as she painted it. This reflection by the child not only sharpens the ability to self-evaluate, a critical skill to develop if independence in learning is desired, but also teaches the child that the consideration of meaning is important in the educational process and that much of this meaning lies within. Moreover, what the child reveals at this point provides valuable information for the teacher to use in reflection.

Implied throughout this description of a child-centred approach to teaching is an emphasis on individual children and their behaviours rather than a view of children as a group. This does not suggest that children always require separate learning activities, though such activities are appropriate from time to time. It does, however, underscore the need to consider how the curriculum is relating to the individual child; only after such a focus on the individuals can the teacher move to summarizing how the group as a whole seems to have fared.

This description of what a child-centred approach to teaching includes thus acknowledges two main themes: the importance of the individual child and the necessity of beginning with children and their behaviours in making all instructional decisions. These themes become clearer in Table 1 which outlines how a child-centred approach to teaching can proceed.

The notion of a child-centred approach to teaching takes on more specific definition when it combines with other elements in the organic curriculum. Recognizing children's view of the world and the way they learn at their stage of development leads the teacher naturally to the need for an experientially-based curriculum which integrates content areas. Considering children's thinking processes and how to encourage them introduces the element of a process-oriented approach to teaching.

The Role of Concrete Experience

If teachers are to behave in reference to what children do, then children must be actively involved in classroom events. If a critical dimension of a child-centred approach to teaching includes teacher response to children's behaviour, then the children must have opportunities to act on their world

Table 1: *The demonstration of a child-centred approach to teaching*

During the planning of what and how to teach	During classroom interaction	During evaluation
1 Consider the needs of children first.	1 Observe carefully children's behaviours which reveal their thinking.	1 Consider what individual children have learned in reference to what was intended for them.
2 Consider children's interests.	2 Respond individually to children's behaviours.	
3 Incorporate children's point of view on classroom events.	3 Provide specific and individual feedback to encourage children's thinking.	2 Involve children in determining the meaning of what was learned.
4 Consider children as individuals who share much in common but who also have specific needs.		

in significant ways so as to provide the teacher with the necessary windows into their current thinking.

Developmental psychology reminds us that children are driven to experience the world by manipulating its objects and by interacting with people important to them. Specifically, Piaget's view stresses not only that concrete experiences are helpful to the learning of children aged seven to twelve but that they are the quintessential building blocks of thinking during this age period. Thinking operations begin with experiences which lead to problem-solving; thus, the child is not limited to the concrete experiences but actively uses them in pursuing ideas and making applications. And, without these experiences, thinking at this stage cannot be developed.

To select appropriate experiences for the classroom, the teacher must consider the quality of those experiences. Experiences differ from each other in several respects. Dale's (1969) 'cone of experience' in figure 1 depicts how various activities distinguish themselves from each other based on their relative position along a continuum from those directly drawn from everyday life to those which use verbal symbols as their primary material for learning.

Using the cone as a point of reference, for example, the teacher may choose to have children visit the countryside to explore the topography of the area, to examine how land forms have evolved and to observe the indigenous wildlife, or the children may instead read about the geography and the animals of a particular area. These two possible approaches represent the diverse experiences available to teachers. Because the consequences for learning can be considerable, teachers of seven to twelve-year-olds are bound to select experiences toward the base of the cone.

The selection of experiences also involves distinguishing among the possibilities in terms of their potential for being educative. Dewey (1938) indirectly describes how educative experiences can be characterized through his account of how experiences can 'go wrong'. His focus is upon how present experiences must foster the quality of future experiences.

> The belief that all genuine education comes about through experience does not mean that all experiences are genuinely or equally educative. Experience and education cannot be directly equated to each other. For some experiences are mis-educative. Any experience is mis-educative that has the effect of arresting or distorting the growth of further experience. An experience may be such as to engender callousness; it may produce lack of sensitivity and of responsiveness. Then the possibilities of having richer experience in the future are restricted. Again, a given experience may increase a person's automatic skill in a particular direction and yet tend to land

Figure 1: The cone of experience

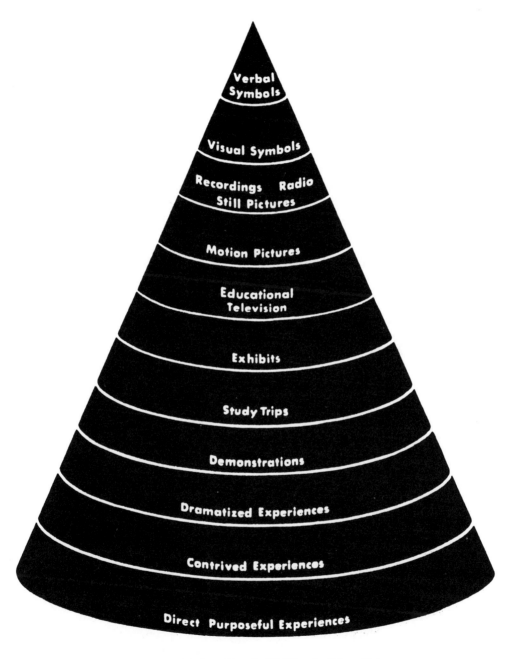

From: *Audiovisual Methods in Teaching,* 3rd Edition, by Edgar Dale.
Copyright © 1946, 1954, 1969 by Holt, Rinehart & Winston, Inc.
Reprinted by permission of CBS College Publishing.

him in a groove or rut; the effect again is to narrow the field of further experience. An experience may be immediately enjoyable and yet promote the formation of a slack and careless attitude; this attitude then operates to modify the quality of subsequent experiences so as to prevent a person from getting out of them what they have to give. Again, experiences may be so disconnected from one another that, while each is agreeable or even exciting in itself, they are not linked cumulatively to one another. Energy is then dissipated and a person becomes scatter-brained. Each experience may be lively, vivid, and 'interesting', and yet their disconnectedness may artificially generate dispersive, disintegrated, centrifugal habits. The consequence of formation of such habits is inability to control future experiences. They are then taken, either by way of enjoyment or of discontent and revolt, just as they come. Under such circumstances, it is idle to talk of self-control. (pp. 25–6)

To extrapolate, Dewey offers a yardstick against which the teacher can measure experiences to determine if they are educative. Educative experiences are those which facilitate future experiences in several ways: by encouraging growth in new areas and by broadening the child's perspective; by promoting rigour, sensitivity and responsiveness so that subsequent work can be richer and deeper; and by fostering deliberate connections among each other.

The teacher can take these guidelines and translate them into a more specific checklist which reflects not only the concern for making experiences educative but also the relationship of the role of experience with the other elements in the organic curriculum. As an example, experiential activities which facilitate learning in the organic curriculum:

1 relate to the interests of the children — both known to them and not yet known to them.
2 relate to the interests and knowledge of the teacher.
3 are based on topics or themes which incorporate many content areas.
4 include many opportunities for communicating through listening, reading, speaking and writing.
5 present situations which encourage children to ask questions.
6 provide opportunities for children to select subtopics of interest to them which then lead to individual research and self-expression.
7 contain the potential for the development of concepts and skills into many areas of learning; that is, act as avenues to future learnings.
8 focus on the processes of observing, making decisions, organizing, creating and evaluating.

9 provide opportunities for both breadth of exposure and depth of investigation.

10 encourage children to be responsible for their own learning through their personal involvement in tasks, their working with materials and their self-evaluation of effort.

Such a checklist emphasizes how the careful selection of educative experiences leads to the inclusion of a child-centred approach to teaching, the integration of content areas and a focus on the development of processes. The elements in the organic curriculum are intimately linked together.

One such educative experience which is appropriate in the organic curriculum could be a teacher-designed display set up in the classroom to depict life in Victorian times. Furniture, tools, books, objets d'art, all allow the child to observe and manipulate so as to promote learning. Such an experience has some limitations since the demonstration of everyday life is static, but there is concreteness and the objects are authentic.

A motorbike brought into the classroom provides yet another opportunity for experience. Its high interest level with children can stimulate questioning which in turn leads to investigations regarding how machines work and their uses in society. With the everyday example before them for careful observation, children are able to follow more easily the steps in mechanical functioning and to determine how one machine part relates to the other parts. The children's experience is a matter of observing and manipulating a real machine very familiar to them in their daily lives.

A half-day visit to a local church is an example of another type of experience. The church itself represents much worthy of direct study — its architecture, the artefacts within it, the surrounding monuments and the symbolic purposes these support. The church also provides experience because it affords opportunities for involvement in its services and for learning about the meaning behind them. As a result, the children place particular real-life objects in a context and examine how people use what they have created to meet their needs.

A visit to a flour mill serves as another example of the range of experiences appropriate for children aged seven to twelve. Even though the mill is no longer in production, it still operates for demonstration purposes; because the children travel to the actual site, they can observe not only how the mill works but also the geographical and economic context which supported it. An experience thereby acquires an added dimension beyond the use of authentic objects in the classroom. The children also can view the steps followed in using tools to produce the flour, a process resulting in an even broader experience.

Clearly, these examples demonstrate that the types of experiences the teacher can select are rich and varied. They differ in their complexity, from observing objects alone in the classroom or in conjunction with related materials in an extensive display to studying the entire operation of a social institution in its human context. Involvement in experiences also makes different demands on time, from convenient observations at frequent intervals during ongoing classroom work to in-depth study on-site for several hours or even several days. However, the experiences always serve as dynamic 'jumping-off' points which lead to diverse activities during which children refer to these 'slices' of everyday life, points which motivate learning and lend clarity to thinking.

Once experiences have been selected, the teacher must design ways to incorporate them into instructional sequences. The role experiences play in the learning process can vary. A useful organizational approach to make instruction experientially-based is one which places the selected experience at the centre of a set of activities. It becomes the starting point from which learning develops in many directions, into many content areas and to deep levels; it serves as a means for initially involving the children in tasks of interest to them and provides opportunities for children to explore these topics actively. In the subsequent work which evolves from the initial experience, the children can use it as a concrete reference, as a way of placing the more symbolic activity into real-life contexts and of connecting it to what they have directly sensed earlier.

One way in which this experiential learning process can occur is in stages which develop from a rich initial experience. The chart which follows explains these stages in greater detail:

Stages of the Experiential Learning Process

Stage I: Identification/involvement with the experience

Here the teacher seeks and then identifies an experience with materials of interest to children which also fulfils guidelines regarding what learning processes are both desirable and necessary for children aged seven to twelve. At this stage the children also become involved with the experience and thereby are committed to pursuing tasks which are indigenous to the experience.

Stage II: Orientation/exploration by means of the experience

The children investigate by means of the experience, examine materials they encounter, determine important questions to ask about the materials and pursue initial data-gathering about the nature of the experience.

Stage III: Acquisition of background

Here the children acquire understanding of the requirements of working with certain topics, materials and tools unique to the experience. Basic skills are sharpened to meet the needs of the tasks

---

being outlined. Research to answer specific questions provides children with perspective on topics.

Stage IV: In-depth investigation

Here the commitment of the children to analysis of materials and topics and to the expression of ideas about them becomes apparent. Intensity of activity, thoroughness and seriousness of effort and intellectual responsibility emerge. Flexibility and time provide the opportunity for this work to develop fully.

Stage V: Closure

Here the children explore meaning and significance with regard to both the topics studied and the work pursued. Contemplation and reflection are encouraged. Work is both valued through sharing and evaluated in terms of the children's own analyses and through the teacher's interpretation of their progress.

These stages become clearer when following an experiential sequence of some eleven-year-olds. In *Stage I*, their teacher carefully studied the learning opportunities which a school field trip to a medieval priory in rural Yorkshire might foster. He chose to use this trip as the pivot around which several topics and themes related to the history and geography of the area could be developed over a period of time upon return to the school.

During the field trip, in *Stage II*, the children walked through the countryside, exercised their skills in observation and map-reading, raised questions about the area's historical background and examined everyday life in the region. The children thereby became actively involved with several complex experiences by completing simple tasks relevant to life in that environment, asking questions about what they saw and did and gathering information regarding the area.

After their return home, the children organized their original impressions by describing in art forms or in writing what they saw at the priory or on their walks. They expanded upon their initial questions and information through historical and scientific background research. Here the *Stage III* activities feed into subsequent *Stage IV* work both by providing basic information and by honing the skills required for *Stage IV* activities to be successful.

In the sequence being described here, the children selected topics to investigate in depth in *Stage IV*, for example, why the area was subject to invasion and the results of those invasions, everyday life in the Middle Ages and how land forms have changed over the centuries in northern England. To pursue such investigations competently, the teacher realized, for example, that the children needed to develop a sense of time with regard to long periods of history and that they needed to become familiar with the many types of land formations observable in the area visited. The children also came to appreciate that reading in the reference books provided for them by the teacher helped to supply the information necessary in answering many of their questions. Thus, children pursued questions of interest to them or expressed with care and detail their observations and their reactions to what they experienced, whether in poetry, descriptive writing, painting, pen and ink or clay work.

After considerable and lengthy work, the children were able to evaluate the quality of what they had accomplished, to describe what they had learned about topics or themes investigated and to assess their own developing skills in observing, experimenting, researching, writing or painting. They shared with their classmates what they had discovered about the topics or themes and about themselves as learners — what was most challenging for them, how they met the challenge and how they felt about their responses. In this way, they reached closure regarding their own long journey into complex areas of human understanding, made exciting, clear and vivid through a concrete, real-life, first-hand, initial experience, to which they could refer throughout the process.

These stages in experiential learning place the child at the centre of education, lead the child naturally to the many traditional content areas of the curriculum and develop the child's abilities in human processes such as observing, questioning, communicating, organizing and creating. Once again, the interrelationships among the elements in the organic curriculum appear to occur spontaneously.

The Integration of Content Areas

The integration of the traditional content areas in the primary school is a central characteristic of the organic curriculum. That is, subjects such as mathematics, language and literacy, art, science, social studies, music and movement are not studied independently but rather are combined in different ways when children are learning.

This process occurs naturally during the first years of life since the tasks of early development represent components of what adults may call science, mathematics, language and so on. A child putting objects in the shapes of squares and circles into their appropriate boxes while talking about what is going on is using language and mathematics at the same time; when the child later throws the square and triangular objects to see if triangles can 'go further', she may be testing her world scientifically.

In addition, the integration of content areas easily occurs in most adult everyday tasks where reading and mathematics skills may be necessary to solve problems involving science or social science concepts. For example, certain employees may complain about working conditions, and their supervisor may respond by reading previous safety reports and examining productivity analyses in order to determine what is causing low morale and less-than-optimum job performance. More simply, integration of content areas is evident when a person bakes a cake and needs to substitute ingredients because the person must read the recipe, must measure amounts and determine equivalence and must consider chemical reactions when changing ingredients so that the final product is edible. There is thus a strong argument that human functioning inherently integrates the subject areas of the traditional school curriculum.

Such a line of thinking can lead to the conclusion that the organization of school curricula around specific disciplines has often occurred for the convenience of the institution rather than because learning requires it. There is, however, a long tradition of integrating subject areas in teaching, particularly with children twelve and younger. Translations of John Dewey's thinking into school practices brought about an emphasis on experiences which paralleled daily life and emphasized problem-solving and thus integrated for children many traditional fields of study. A version of this approach has been labelled the 'unit method of teaching' in which the many subjects of the curriculum are studied in reference to a central topic or theme; this idea serves as a connecting link among all subject areas, and all work pursued relates deliberately to it. Presently, some teachers are adopting an integrated approach to teaching because they see it as an efficient way to handle the many demands within the pressurized curriculum and as an avenue to offer many opportunities for the application of learnings.

The concept of integration has many meanings. Simply stated, integration of content areas means that what could be separated is kept together or what has been separated is now mixed or combined so that the curriculum experience of children is interrelated. The parts remain attached or are brought together again because they are related to each other and because the main idea they share becomes thereby clearer.

There are many ways in which this integration occurs in the teaching of children aged seven to twelve. Several of these variations follow. The purpose of describing these forms of integrated teaching is to stress the many ways in which the traditional content areas can relate to each other during ongoing instruction; the accompanying sketches in figures 2 through 7 demonstrate in visual terms the nature of these relationships.

1 The *incidental approach* to integration occurs while the focus is on a traditional content emphasis in the curriculum. It appears when enrichment activities are included during instruction, and it is often demonstrated when a teacher brings in a wide range of examples.

Such an approach to integration provides teachers with the opportunity to include certain content areas when financial and time constraints may otherwise dictate their elimination from the daily timetable.

Figure 2:   The incidental approach to integration

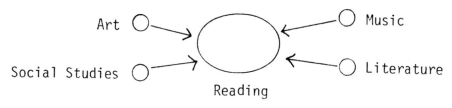

Examples: When a child is reading and meets the word 'azure' in the course of a story, the teacher explains how this shade of blue differs from other shades of blue. To do this, the teacher relates the word to the child's experiences of mixing colour during painting. When a child reads to the teacher and the teacher and child then discuss the meaning of what is read, it can lead to a deeper understanding of the subject under discussion, whether it be the seaside, birds of prey or whatever.

2 *Reinforcement and practice* provide applications in other content areas of what has been taught in one content area. This approach is particularly evident when children use language and mathematics skills during their work in other subject areas. Reinforcement and practice can also be means by which children's skills are extended into successful experiences in curriculum areas where they may not be confident. In this way, the reinforcement and practice facilitate learning in the other curriculum areas.

Figure 3:   Integration during reinforcement and practice

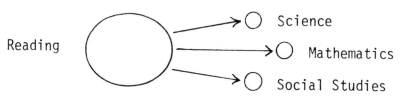

Examples: The development of information-gathering skills, often presented as part of the language curriculum, gains meaning as the child uses these skills in answering science or social studies questions. Graphing skills, acquired during mathematics instruction, become relevant when organizing data recorded in social studies or science. And, movement skills may be used in activities which actually demonstrate certain concepts as part of vocabulary development in reading.

3 With *embedding*, one content area is placed 'into' another. Some examples of embedding occur when teachers include vocabulary development during a movement lesson or an art activity as a part of a social studies lesson.

Figure 4:   Integration through embedding

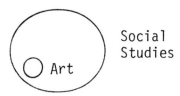

Social
Studies

Art

Examples: Children may model mountain ranges out of clay in order to develop an understanding of form and shape and their relationship to land formation. Children may also paint people in Victorian costumes within appropriate settings as a means to acquire a better understanding of social history. In both cases, the art elements are still important parts of the learning activity even as that art activity is serving the needs of another part of the curriculum.

4 *Coordination* of work in two separate content areas occurs when certain topics in common are consciously related to each other and are actually presented in conjunction with each other. This approach reflects the juxtaposition of individual concepts or generalizations in various subject areas when appropriate so that they can be taught together.

Figure 5:   Integration through coordination

History   Literature

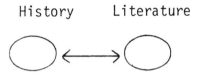

Example: Historical facts about Victorian England and generalizations regarding the causes and effects of the Industrial Revolution are deliberately paired with study of Dickens in literature. The concurrent study in one content area supports study in the other area.

5 The integration of content areas may involve an emphasis on *process objectives*. That is, integration occurs when activities are drawn from several content areas for the purpose of promoting the growth of processes such as observing, organizing or communicating, or in order to develop critical thinking skills. The organizing principle for integration here is the promotion of growth in process skills or the development of thinking skills across the curriculum.

Figure 6:   Integration through processes

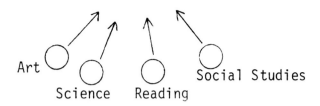

Example: Throughout all parts of the curriculum, a teacher identifies opportunities for observational skills to be developed; therefore, a display of flowers might be studied with regard to line, space or colour, as well as with regard to the flowers' botanical structure. In mathematics, measuring activities mean selecting the appropriate instrument and looking at it carefully when carrying out the measurement tasks. Later that same day, the teacher might have children observe likenesses and similarities in handwriting samples to determine the factors contributing to legibility.

6 A *topic or thematic organization* starts with real-life problems, centres of interests and questions from the children which are not discipline-specific and which therefore incorporate integration automatically as activities are designed in response. The topic or theme naturally leads to work in a variety of traditional content areas. The organization of the activities is driven by the nature of the topic or theme and not by the nature of the disciplines.

Example: A farm visit leads to work in natural science, reading, art and writing, among others, as that work supports the expansion of children's understanding of the farm life topic or theme.

The examples above depict how daily teaching can be integrated. However, integration of the traditional content areas also becomes important when one examines how the curriculum as a whole may be organized over time. Three approaches seem possible here, from one which

Figure 7:   Integration using topic or thematic organization

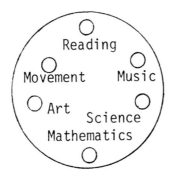

keeps the disciplines relatively separate and individually identifiable to one which merges areas so that the topics or themes become the focus of attention. Following is an outline of how these approaches might be differentiated.

I. *The Introduce — Focus — Reinforce Approach*

The teacher:

1 Builds awareness of a skill or concept in other content areas. Background is presented in other areas; exposure is offered in an incidental way.

2 Focuses on developing the skill or concept within the content area where it is 'traditionally' placed.

3 Reinforces the skill or concept in other content areas by providing many and varied opportunities for practice.

Example: When developing map-reading abilities, the teacher explains the map directions of north, south, east and west when they are mentioned in stories, or he points out an island on a map to pair with a description of an island in a poem or he places on a map points discussed in the daily news. Later, the teacher has the children construct scale drawings of the classroom or school or work with real maps when studying peoples around the world in order to develop the ability to interpret maps accurately. As the third step in this approach, the children make maps in preparation for a school visit or use available maps to determine itineraries.

II. *The Interactive Approach* which combines areas by means of their connecting strands or threads

The teacher:

1 Identifies where certain skills and concepts are already being taught in different content areas.

2 Plans how to teach these together to stress the interrelatedness of

material, to use time effectively and to compare examples. Figure 8 indicates how a teacher may connect certain skills and concepts taught in various content areas.

Figure 8: Connecting skills and concepts across content areas

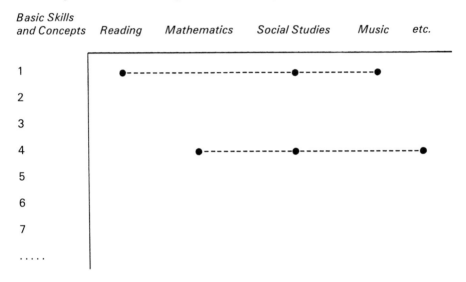

Example: Measurement is developed across several areas in the curriculum as a theme represented by rhythm in music, by number in mathematics, by time in social studies, with the latter two used in science experiments. The teacher thus ensures the children develop a broadly based concept of measurement.

III. *The Topic or Thematic Approach* which merges content areas in order to create a single focus

The teacher:

1 Identifies a topic or theme which relates to life experiences or to the interests of children.

2 Organizes the sequence of activities here so that important skills and concepts are developed while exploring the topic or theme.

Example: The children study: 'Our Green Kingdom', which incorporates work traditionally associated with science, mathematics, social studies, health and language; 'Meteorology', which includes work associated with science, geography, mathematics, language and art; or 'The Use of Machines', which encompasses work in history and geography (the Industrial Revolution), economics, science (physics) and mathematics, language and art.

In order for teachers and schools to integrate the traditional content areas effectively, they must ascribe to certain beliefs. Some of these are:

1 The school's responsibility is to educate the 'whole' child who is developing in skills, in thought and in attitude.
2 The purpose of education is to develop children's abilities in observing, categorizing, communicating, questioning, critical thinking and evaluating. That is, teachers believe in 'process education'.
3 Evaluation is a matter of assessing growth in general cognitive and affective processes and not just monitoring discrete skill acquisition in particular content areas.
4 Experiences are the means through which integration of the traditional content areas easily occurs. They are not only effective motivators of learning but are necessary in terms of the developmental stages of children's learning.
5 Basic skills such as reading and mathematics are best developed and practiced in the context of a broad curriculum requiring children to apply those skills in a variety of situations.

Without the support of these beliefs, it is likely that integration will remain a superficial endeavour.

Of course, certain conditions within the school can make the process of integrating the curriculum easier. They include:

1 Sharing among staff members engaged in integrating the curriculum for mutual support, encouragement and inspiration;
2 A self-contained classroom pattern in school organization or one which supports a team approach so that coordination among staff members who teach the various subjects can occur easily;
3 The use of a wide variety of materials as primary learning resources which simultaneously represent many content areas;
4 The adoption of a long-term view of curriculum change so that integration of content can be undertaken slowly but positively;
5 Viewing the process of curriculum change as developmental and evolutionary, with each step pursued after the previous step is solidly in practice;
6 Time and opportunity for teachers to reflect on the process of integration for purposes of self-evaluation and growth;
7 Support for the professional decision-making of teachers in the classroom who are best able to determine the nature of the learning experiences appropriate for a given group of children.

Rethinking the curriculum to integrate content areas is a demanding process which requires much not only of those people who do it but also of the individuals who support their efforts.

This analysis of what is necessary for integrating the curriculum effectively also reminds us that the key elements of the organic curriculum tend to appear together. For integration to be a dynamic force in learning, it must be accompanied by rich experiences which emphasize the processes critical to children's intellectual growth and which meet children's interests and needs.

The integration of the content areas is a key characteristic of the organic curriculum because it complements experiential learning and supports a child-centred approach to teaching. Indeed, integration appears almost unavoidable if the curriculum is focused upon connecting learning to real-life tasks, either through the use of experiences or by means of stressing the application of skills and concepts. Moreover, when content areas are integrated, the potential for learning increases both because children become highly involved and because the many possible connections among skills and concepts are reinforced.

A Process Approach to Teaching

As implied earlier, a notion complementary to the integration of content areas is a process approach to teaching. Central here is the assumption that growth in exercising basic human processes is a principal purpose of the school. This exercise of specific human processes — for example, observing, comparing, questioning, decision-making, experimenting — enables children to learn actively and to see connections among areas of human endeavour. In this way, they also acquire the necessary concrete experiences from which more abstract learning may develop.

There are several conceptualizations in the literature of a process approach to teaching. Current emphases on the development of critical thinking skills also reflect a concern for process, although the focus is generally upon cognitive functioning alone. The stress here is that a process orientation in teaching involves a valuing of all forms of learning: cognitive, affective and psychomotor. The school accepts the child as a fully functioning individual who will grow in all areas of human competence.

Berman's view (1968) provides a broad perspective on what a process approach to teaching can mean. She identifies what she calls eight basic process skills which all people can exhibit: perceiving, communicating, loving, decision-making, knowing, organizing, creating and valuing. The school's task is to plan experiences through which persons can become more skilled in these processes. These processes extend into all areas of the school curriculum and thus can be central to the structure of that curriculum.

Berman presents several ways for using that structure to organize school learnings. One method acknowledges common processes as children encounter them in various content areas, as when children compare communication methods in language activities and later in mathematics. A different approach has children focus on a given process, such as decision-making, and examine it as it is used in different content areas such as social studies, science and language. Berman, therefore, works with the content emphases of the school and uses processes as a focus for learning and as a means for integrating the content areas.

How one defines the particular processes a curriculum develops appears to be less important than the acknowledgement that the development of processes is a key element in children's learning. As a result, while teachers who view the curriculum as process-oriented may identify different lists of processes from time to time, they will always recognize that children's behaviours are central to their own thinking about instruction. They will then begin with an emphasis upon what the child can do in order to encourage further growth.

The process approach to teaching in the organic curriculum shares much in common with Bermans's conceptualization. It too views children as already possessing many process skills which grow and develop as their experiences expand. Here teachers select learning activities for children which provide opportunities for demonstrating and perfecting particular processes. Some examples are shown in Table 2. Teachers, therefore, consciously appreciate the connections between the activities they design and the processes those activities develop.

The organic curriculum's stress on processes seems to require particular teaching practices. The list in Table 3 identifies certain important processes and indicates what the teacher needs to do in order to foster their development. This outline suggests that considering processes as a key element in the organic curriculum necessitates a child-centred approach to teaching which is experientially-based and which integrates traditional content areas. As before, the central characteristics appear to be interdependent and mutually supportive.

The Role of Basic Skills

A starting point for discussion is the assertion that the basic skills of the curriculum must be broadly defined so that they include not only reading and mathematics but also other language skills and the fundamental ways of functioning effectively in the other areas of the curriculum. Indeed, the

Table 2:   Activities and processes in the organic curriculum

Activities in the organic curriculum	Processes involved in these activities
drawing/painting/sculpting	comparing/contrasting
construction/problem-solving	observing using materials/tools organizing/designing/patterning making decisions
discussion of ideas/sharing results	listening reflecting organizing expressing
experimenting	observing collecting information organizing summarizing
writing	using reference sources predicting reflecting organizing selecting making decisions connecting ideas analyzing component parts expressing oneself creatively evaluating

process orientation of the organic curriculum provides a framework for considering the nature of basic skills. The organic curriculum views processes in addition to reading, writing and the mastery of mathematics as equally basic, for example, the abilities of children to observe closely their environment, to gather information, to record and organize data, to express clearly their thinking and to relate ideas to each other.

Consideration of basic skills must also acknowledge that there are many types of knowledge included in the school curriculum. Traditionally, the content areas have served to group the various facts, concepts and generalizations deemed important by society for the young to learn. Some of these content areas emphasize what are termed basic skills more than others; but since these content areas are intimately connected to all the other areas, such skills are developed in the context of pursuing all types of knowledge.

Another way to proceed in considering the role of basic skills in the organic curriculum is to identify how such skills are addressed when the curriculum is in action. The example which follows demonstrates how the stages of the experiential learning process presented earlier include emphases on significant skills.

Sample Skills Involved at Various Stages of the Experiential Learning Process

Stage I: Identification/involvement with the experience
— identification of interests
— acknowledgement of individual academic strengths and weaknesses

Stage II: Orientation/exploration by means of the experience
— formulation of questions
— question-asking — orally
— initial information-gathering through listening and reading
— discussing

Stage III: Acquisition of background
— development of research skills and skills in working with specialized materials and tools, including mathematics materials
— question-asking — orally and in writing
— information-gathering through listening and reading
— comparing and contrasting — orally, in writing and in mathematics
— summarizing

Stage IV: In-depth investigation
— application of information to problem-solving tasks.
— analysis of materials and ideas — orally, in writing and in mathematics
— expressing and synthesizing — orally, in small groups, in writing and in mathematics

Stage V: Closure
— summarizing
— expressing and synthesizing — orally, in small and large groups, in writing and in mathematics
— answering questions
— evaluation of materials and experiences
— self-evaluation of skills attained and learnings acquired

Because much current professional literature discusses the need for developing the basic skills of reading and mathematics among children aged seven to twelve, one must consider how the organic curriculum fulfils this responsibility of the school. It is necessary to acknowledge that from time to time isolated skill development in mathematics and reading is desirable. For example, the acquisition of certain number skills prior to their application within a thematic approach may be appropriate. Similarly, it may be appropriate for a child with a 'block' in mathematics to concentrate on

Table 3:   Processes and teaching practices in the organic curriculum

Processes developed in the organic curriculum	Teaching practices which facilitate growth in these processes
observing and perceiving	provision of experiential base to learning
decision-making	presentation of structured and meaningful choices
using materials and locating information	provision of active and concrete learning tasks; placing basic skills in context
knowing/encountering and processing information	provision of rich environment with many stimuli; asking questions; provision of active and concrete learning tasks
making connections/organizing one's knowledge	integration of curriculum; placing basic skills in context
communicating	having children share what is learned with others; encouraging children to work constructively with others in carrying out learning tasks
expressing ideas	provision of opportunities for synthesizing learning in written, oral and artistic forms
valuing	encouraging children's own evaluation of the quality of their work; developing in children responsibility for their own learning, respect for others and care for the learning environment

certain skills in that area only as these may assist in the development and expansion of both knowledge and confidence. However, this emphasis on skills in a particular part of the curriculum must be in the context of child-centred and experientially-based activities which also stress the importance of the wide range of human processes. While integration of the content areas may not occur all of the time, it is crucial that the other elements of the organic curriculum be carefully acknowledged in order to give meaning and validity to the skills being acquired.

Therefore, the critical concern of the organic curriculum is how to develop effectively the many basic skills in the context of a child-centred, process-oriented approach to teaching which emphasizes the role of concrete experiences in learning and the integration of content areas over time. Clearly, this curriculum supports the premise that the greatest growth in the broadly defined basic skills occurs when they are intertwined with experiences and are addressed during the process of work which integrates the content areas and responds to children's interests and needs.

Combining the Elements

While the previous discussion has attempted to lay out the key elements of the organic curriculum separately, their interrelationships have also been apparent throughout. The organic curriculum is a complex, dynamic enterprise. The accompanying diagram in Figure 9 displays how the elements interact during the functioning of the organic curriculum.

Each element participates in influencing the whole of the process of organic teaching and learning; each element is necessary to the whole, and

Figure 9:   The learning sequence in the organic curriculum

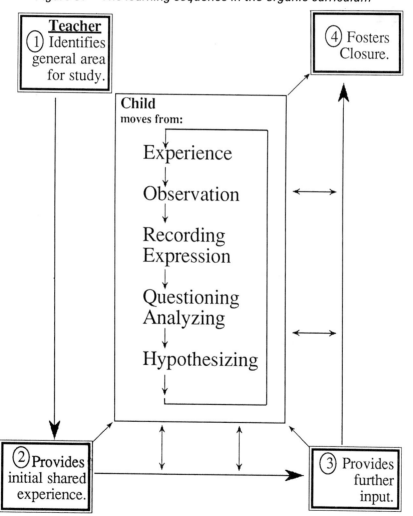

all elements must work together to produce the whole. But the total picture reflects an integrated view which represents more than just the sum of the component parts.

While it is difficult to conceptualize precisely what is meant when the elements are combined to form the organic curriculum, it is possible to suggest the implications of such an approach for the role of the teacher. Adherence to a child-centred, process-oriented approach to teaching which acknowledges the role of concrete experience and the importance of integrating the content areas means that the teacher becomes a designer of experiences, an initiator of activities, an observer of children's behaviours, a facilitator of growth in processes and a guide to children as they become responsible, independent, reflective learners. How the elements of the organic curriculum and the concomitant role of the teacher demonstrate themselves in specific practices is the focus of the next chapter.

Part II
The Nature of the Organic Curriculum

Chapter 4

Observing the Learning Process

This chapter both describes and analyzes how the elements of the organic curriculum presented in Chapter 3 work together in actual class situations. It offers several scenarios drawn from extended observational experiences with teachers and children which demonstrate organic teaching and learning in action. It also discusses how each scenario reflects an integrated approach to the curriculum which is child-centred, experientially based and process-oriented.

The examples illustrate both the range of possibilities available within the context of an organic curriculum and the diverse ways in which teachers can work with children in order to accomplish desired goals. Through the descriptions and analyses, it will also become apparent that the organic curriculum effectively develops the essential skills in language and mathematics needed by children while confronting fundamental concepts and generalizations representative of the disciplines of knowledge included in the primary school.

Central to the organic curriculum are the relationships between teacher and children and among the children themselves which direct and nurture the process of learning. As a result, the examples chosen of class practice also demonstrate the nature of these relationships and how they may develop.

The examples also describe the role of the environment throughout the learning process. Not only is the physical setting an important support in the organic curriculum, but also the materials and tools which teachers and children use to foster learning. Suggesting how teachers and children structure the setting and select and work with the necessary materials and tools contributes to an understanding of the fully functioning organic curriculum.

The following descriptions and analyses reflect the perspective of the teacher with regard to the organization and functioning of the working classroom. This is not because the perspective of the child is not important; as stressed earlier, a child-centred curriculum indeed demands that the teacher constantly incorporate the child's point of view when making professional decisions. The purpose at this point, however, is to offer close analysis of the interactions and activities observed in the organic classroom so that teachers might be better able to focus tightly on its four elements and thereby reflect on teaching and practice.

To facilitate the processes of close description and analysis, the chapter adopts the view of a highly interested outsider to the school who observes class interactions and activities over a substantial period of time and provides an interpretive narration. Thus, the observer's point of view leads the reader to a detached and perhaps more informative account of life within the organic curriculum. Further, the view represents what an observer with quite different professional and social experiences may see in a school setting both similar to and yet very different from school life elsewhere.

In each of the views of the organic curriculum in action to follow, there is description of particular events; the reader thus encounters school life much as the careful observer sees it. However, rather than an extensive description of a wide variety of events which a tour of the school might reveal, only a few are highlighted in order to permit greater discussion of how each relates to the teacher's curricular decision-making. The discussion of what has been observed as teachers and children work together therefore includes accounts of the context of these events, both in the temporal sense and in terms of stages within the overall process of learning, along with interpretive asides. The interpretation and analysis elucidate the behaviours through attention to the role the four elements of the organic curriculum play, the nature of the interpersonal relationships and the interaction of the teacher and children with materials and tools. Throughout this process, the intent is to sharpen understanding of what the organic curriculum is striving to accomplish while retaining much of its complexity. Only with the achievement of such a tight focus may one begin to appreciate how to implement this approach to teaching.

Children of Ten and Eleven Years

If one were to take observational snapshots around a school which follows the organic curriculum, many kinds of interactions and activities would emerge. One would be struck by the sheer energy of both teachers and children, by the use of a wide variety of materials, by the hum of work being confidently and responsibly carried out by children who clearly understand their tasks, by the high quality of children's accomplishment representing many curriculum areas and by the good humour and positive feelings of all in the school. However, in order to understand deeply the functioning of the organic curriculum, one must look closely and carefully while simultaneously reflecting and interpreting.

In one classroom, for instance, a teacher and twenty-seven ten-year-olds focus on work growing out of an earlier visit to a nineteenth-century flour mill. During the initial morning instructional period, lasting about an hour and a quarter, some children are writing descriptions of how the mill looks, how it works or what different workers used to do. Other children depict various aspects of the external appearance of the mill in paint, pen and ink, pencil or sewing on fabric; still others, using much accurate detail in their illustration, show numerous figures working in the mill, parts of machines in operation or the many activities of the mill. Some children are examining slides of the mill taken during the visit, while others who are cooperatively constructing a clay model of the mill demonstrate the poses of workers in order to determine how the equipment functions.

The teacher moves around the classroom and consults with individuals and groups about the progress of their work. With one child, she suggests a medium of expression, and with another she offers clear specific feedback about what she sees in the drawing as well as exploring with the child possible ways to expand the detail. At another time, the teacher reviews with a child how parts of the mill work in order to help him clarify his written explanation of the mill's operation.

In responding to a painting, she asks one girl, 'How are you going to show the stones on the building? What do you need to do? How could you do it? What are the advantages of each way you are thinking of using?' After each question, the child appears to be mulling thoughts over in her mind and offers some initial ideas. The teacher nods and then leaves the child with the task of attacking the problem presented.

These children have been working in similar environments for several years. They therefore have implicit expectations about what activities are part of school life, what procedures they should follow both in preparing for the activities and in carrying them out, what teachers generally do to get them started and to help them along as they work and how they should look at what they themselves have done in order to ask questions, assess progress and acquire some sense of meaningfulness about the work. These children have also been working with this particular class teacher for several months so they are familiar with her style of questioning, of offering feedback and of contributing suggestions. In short, there has been time for teacher and children to learn how to work together smoothly, easily and confidently.

The pace of interaction is measured and deliberate, assuring that the necessary time is spent clarifying tasks, carefully carrying them out and reflecting on what has occurred in order to chart the next steps. There is little concern for producing a certain quantity of work, but rather an emphasis on doing all that may be possible to guarantee that children understand and internalize what is happening. The teacher does, however, ascertain that the children are indeed progressing in their work by sorting out confusion if it arises or by nudging gently those who may need encouragement or structure.

Observing this kind of activity in the classroom for a limited period of time tends to obscure the detailed preparation which the teacher gave the children in order to 'get them started'. Aside from the obvious first-hand experience gained on the visit to the mill, the teacher established a clear context and rationale for the activities in the classroom, discussed the procedures for them in detail with the children and assisted the children in identifying both the relevant experiences and appropriate materials to draw upon in carrying out the activities. Without such a grounding, children could not be expected to function as thoughtfully and confidently as they do.

Later that day, the teacher outlines further work for the children to pursue as they capitalize on the various strands of experience they confronted on the mill visit. In the 'quiet bay', a carpeted area in a corner of the classroom where the children can sit casually, she asks the children to recall the smells and sounds of the mill and to connect these to the way in which people worked in the mill. She also plays an audiotape made during their visit. After discussion of the possibilities for their writing, some of the children begin descriptive poetry while others develop stories.

In this sequence the experience base of the activities is clear. Child-centredness is evident to the extent that there are options for children's work and a recognition that first-hand experience is more likely to generate interest in the topics and concepts presented in the classroom. The teacher, however, is firmly directing the children's efforts towards particular goals, in this case the use of descriptive vocabulary drawing on the senses in prose or poetry. Integration of content areas is also apparent since the language work brings with it a heightened sense of life in another time and of occupations no longer pursued. The resulting development of children's abilities to express themselves clearly and with an effect on the reader reveals a process orientation; what they learn here is applicable in many other contexts as they grow in their ability to communicate.

The next morning the teacher guides the children in organizing their time by reviewing the several activities already introduced in which they need to continue work. Their choice depends upon where they are in their work, the availability of the materials and tools they need to use and the requirement to make steady progress in all of their various tasks. The teacher then resumes her pattern of individual consultation. She suggests to one child how to make a poetry line clearer through altering word choice, notes particularly colourful passages in a story for another or directs yet another to locate information explaining in greater detail how the working conditions in the flour mills affected workers' health which may contribute to plot development in his story. Frequently in her discussion with children, the teacher shares her own thought processes as she works with an idea and how to express it effectively.

In this pattern of work the teacher is building upon her initial, very careful introduction of the tasks. There is no presumption, however, that this preparatory introduction alone suffices to carry the children through in their execution of work. The teacher fully expects to assist children in further defining their individual variations on the generally set task. This assistance may occur shortly after the beginning of their work, as well as later when the children reach decision points affecting the direction of their efforts. As the example here illustrates, the teacher may also individually explain material which relates to the content of what a particular child is writing or may refer others to resource materials to clarify their understanding if the information is central to their development of ideas. While the result of such differentiation in exposure to content may be that some children have acquired a more detailed knowledge of how the mill works or what working conditions were like, in comparison to other children, this additional information is seen as the expansion of work into optional or enrichment areas of the curriculum. Whether or not to attain a clear understanding of the focus of one's writing is not an option for the child, however, since this is the obligation of every writer to the reader. In a sense, then, there is a strong commonality of process during the children's writing experiences even though the focus of the process may lead to some differentiation in their exposure to content.

This attention to process recognizes that the quality of the experience in carrying out a task may be more important in learning than the generation of a product. Such a view is even shared with the children so that they may understand why they are doing what they are doing and how particular steps in a task fit together into a whole. Further, when the development of processes becomes the focus, as in this example, there is a natural integration of curriculum areas; with an emphasis on quality language work children will need to concentrate also on the clarity and accuracy of the ideas from science and social studies which they wish to communicate.

As the teacher consults with the children, she varies the amount of structure provided as they work. This is a further way of differentiating the learning experiences of children. Because she considers how a child's learning style differs from others and how that individual's personality may affect the learning process, her approach may be called child-centred in the most fundamental way. As a result, she is specific in her suggestions to one child and indicates the particular next step he needs to follow with a short range timeline attached, while merely noting to another that a passage may need some rethinking. The teacher of course desires that all children reach the point where they can readily evaluate their own work, determine the direction and extent of their progress in comparison to set goals and function independently of the teacher once activities have been initiated. All children, however, are not at the same stage in their development of these processes, and the teacher acknowledges this reality by both adjusting the nature of her assistance to them and directing them step-by-step toward these long-range goals.

In the classroom after the midday meal, the children read silently from the books they have each selected from the school's collection. This collection has been coded to help the children select books they are capable of reading with only minimal help from a teacher. While the children read for this thirty-minute period, the teacher works with a few individually. She asks one child to read several short sections of his book quickly so as to identify any decoding problems he may be having and to help him develop expressiveness in reading aloud.

For approximately five to ten minutes the teacher discusses with another child what she has been reading. The questions the teacher asks focus on a listing of the main characters, a capsule description of the sequence of events and a statement of why the girl agreed with a decision a main character made at a certain point in the story. It is clear that a wide range of reading tasks are important in this classroom. Though they are developed and practiced in the course of other learning activities, they are also emphasized during a set period when children read quality literature and appropriate non-fiction. The fundamental nature of reading abilities demands such focus.

The way in which the teacher asks a child questions is similar to the tone people take when they are curious about what others know regarding a subject and want to invite them to share their knowledge and thoughts about it; there is no atmosphere of quizzing or judging the responses. With clarification of questions when necessary and through the teacher's non-verbal responses and natural elaboration of ideas, the communication between teacher and child becomes an intimate conversation. This dialogue is genuine and offers the opportunity for the two people to get to know each other better.

The verbal discussion between the teacher and the child, along with the child's reading aloud to the teacher, also allows for diagnosis of the child's progress in the development of a variety of reading comprehension skills. The assessment of these skills is kept in context as is their development.

The quality of the personal relationship which evolves facilitates the other, more role-defined interactions in the classroom and makes it more likely for the child to accept the teacher's direction even when situations become difficult. In the latter category are those actions and statements of teachers designed to refocus children's attention to the task at hand, to have them cease doing something which may be harmful to themselves or others or to cause them to consider the rights of others in a group working environment. If the teacher and Paul have talked together about some important ideas suggested by his reading and she has given him her total attention and some thought-provoking questions, Paul will likely develop respect for her both as an individual and as a person who has responsibility for the learning of a group of children. He will respond more positively than he might have otherwise when she remarks, 'Paul, there are people writing. I think maybe you ought to get on with your writing, quietly'. Within the context of many personal interactions, Paul will interpret this suggestion as a way to encourage work and not as a challenge to his individuality. He knows that respect is mutual between teacher and child and that there are no double standards when it comes to valuing others' integrity within the school.

The teacher does not hesitate to express her anger if an event warrants it. For example, earlier that day a group of children were punching each other in a playful way and consequently broke the point of one of the pens used in drawing. Her response was controlled and yet clear: 'I'm cross. I'm not cross that you have broken it. I'm cross because of the way you broke it'. This teacher not only is genuine in her reaction but also explains why she is reacting in such a way. The children, therefore, will likely see the teacher as a real human being with definite values and one who also respects them enough to control her anger and to explain the reasons for it. She becomes then a model for the children in the healthy expression of emotions while being sensitive to others.

This case also makes it clear that caring for tools is important and that silliness is not appropriate, although accidents may happen legitimately. Norms for acceptable behaviour are reinforced without making the individuals feel attacked personally. They know what they can and cannot do to stay within the limits of behaviour supported by the school. The multiple goals of the organic curriculum are always the key to the careful decision-making of the teacher as she determines how to respond to a given situation.

In a more demanding case later that afternoon, the teacher decides to discuss a child's behaviour with him privately while the other children continue to work. One boy has not been progressing in his classroom tasks for several days. The teacher shares with him what she observed and the fact that she is concerned about his inability to budget time carefully. She invites

Keith to offer his observations of how he has been working, what has been distracting him and what he has accomplished. They then discuss the consequences which will likely occur if behaviour continues in the same vein and what might happen if behaviour were altered. The teacher negotiates a course of action with Keith and establishes an agreement regarding his work pattern for the next day at the end of which they will talk again.

The teacher guides and directs this exchange but also realizes that the child must examine the situation carefully and receive recognition of his perceptions if any meaningful change in behaviour is likely to occur. While her authority operates clearly, the child also influences the outcomes. They select a timeframe of one day because it makes the attempt at a new approach manageable and yet allows the child to handle a significant amount of time independently with only occasional teacher monitoring; it also establishes a point for joint evaluation in an objective climate rather than as a result of a crisis in behaviour.

Even in this emotional, potentially charged interaction, the teacher in the organic curriculum values the importance of developing relationships with children. Because their point of view is central to establishing any new authentic patterns of behaviour, child-centredness in decision-making is essential. Without their involvement, commitment and understanding, behaviour will likely only change to meet external pressure and will disappear when that pressure is removed. Further, there will be little support for the organic curriculum's emphasis on developing children's decision-making capabilities and thus a rational independence in behaviour.

Although one might criticize these concerns for children directing their own behaviour, it is nonetheless apparent that decision-making and independence are valued by society at large as well. The teacher also assumes that these abilities need to be directly nurtured just as with any other part of the curriculum. As a result, the teacher thinks through the many available techniques for handling class interactions and selects an approach which not only addresses the immediate situation but also fosters long-range development in the self-management of behaviour.

A visit to a class of younger children may help put into perspective what is occurring in this group of ten and eleven-year-olds. Many of the children just observed have operated in this way for several years. They are relatively at ease in settings typical of the organic curriculum even though they are tackling more complex learning tasks. How a teacher works with eight-year-olds may help to suggest the approaches which establish children's working patterns and develop their basic skills so that they can later be relatively independent of the teacher, thoughtful and confident in their activity.

Children of Eight and Nine Years

The eight and nine-year-old children in this class have been at this school for five months. They have learned many basic procedures necessary to the operation of a smoothly functioning environment. They seem comfortable in pursuing tasks actively and eagerly. Most of them have come here with a school experience which promotes similar goals for children's learning.

The teacher talks with the children about what they have been doing so far this morning. He notes, 'We've had some of you doing investigations in the activity area on what sounds different objects make when struck, and we've had some children using simple instruments to make their own music. There has been some good work. Now I want you to listen carefully to some music composed by someone else.'

The teacher provides a review of the children's activities and gives them some temporary closure while he also establishes a connection with the activity he is about to introduce. Because the children will return to their work later, they need to assess informally where they now are as a group. They also need help in making connections among class activities so the teacher discusses them directly. He models a thinking process for the children which they can use later in seeing relationships among parts of the curriculum so that school tasks might be seen as sensible and meaningful.

He plays sections of a recording of the 'William Tell Overture' for the children and focuses their listening on the different kinds of sounds they hear and the different 'speeds' in the music. After they have listened to these excerpts, he asks them to describe the various sounds that they heard. Using follow-up questions, the teacher encourages the children to list as many words which vividly depict specific sound qualities as possible and to discuss any ideas which these sounds might suggest through association — standing on a mountain, riding a horse, being chased. Throughout the process, he has them expand their ideas. He shares what he heard, as well, which in turn stimulates further description from the children.

The teacher further sets the scene for the children's writing of a story by again recapping what they have already done with the music. He has them consider what actions the music might be describing and to think about how these actions might be connected in story form. The teacher also suggests how the children can direct their writing so as to avoid some of the difficulties they have encountered in past efforts; for example, he cautions them not to get 'muddled' in the middle of a story with too much going on and to use only a few characters.

This careful introduction of a writing task clearly exhibits the several elements of the organic curriculum. Firstly the integration of content areas occurs quite smoothly. The music as stimulus leads to writing which embodies many goals in language study, all connected in complex ways to the children's earlier experiences in scientifically exploring the nature of sound. The children have thus had several planned encounters with sound which give them solid reference points as they undertake the current writing task.

The process of writing is receiving direct attention, as well, both by the very definition of the task and through the teacher's structuring of the children's work from the pre-writing stage to the writing stage which will later connect to the revision stage. The teacher's acknowledgement of difficulties they might face also underscores the process dimension for the children. They thereby appreciate the cyclical nature of their work in many areas of the curriculum and the active role they can play in directing their own development of competence, characteristics central to any process-oriented experience.

Also pervasive in these interactions is a sense of child-centredness. The teacher provides experiences which are understandable within the children's world view and recognizes the children's stages of intellectual development. His assistance in organizing their work and his simple reminders of useful procedures learned in past efforts underscore an appreciation for how these children are presently thinking.

The easy sharing by the teacher of his thoughts about the music does much to build class relationships. His contributions are offered as a group member, someone who has significant responsibilities here to be sure, but not someone whose ideas are inherently more legitimate than the children's because of that role. The sharing promotes a few moments in which the children can see into the mind of their teacher and thus offers a chance at human closeness. The cumulative effect of these opportunities is to build a strong foundation for teacher-child interaction in all areas of the organic curriculum, including situations which may be stressful.

The afternoon session that day begins with children continuing their work on a variety of tasks. Some are carrying on with the story writing begun earlier while others are exploring arithmetic processes with an abacus, writing up their observations of their investigations with drums and sound or painting a castle described in a story they have been reading together. The teacher observes the children and consults with them as they work, frequently encouraging them to think about what they are going to do: 'Perhaps in this section you can tie some of this together.' . . . 'Perhaps you should reread what you've written before you go on.' . . . 'Can you think about what you are going to do to show the storminess in the sky behind the castle?' . . . 'You've reread what you've written now. Have you decided where the story is going to go?' In each case, he looks at what the children are doing and then helps them organize their work and offers them specific feedback.

This typical scene demonstrates several points. Quite obviously many different kinds of activities are going on in the class simultaneously, even with these children in their first year at the school. They are gaining individual experience in organizing their time and pacing their work and implicitly accept the need for flexibility in accommodating the demands of different types of tasks and variations in workstyle. Time seems to be used carefully and consciously without the clock taking over the process of decision-making.

The teacher structures his role in light of the children's work. He closely observes and analyzes how they are proceeding with their tasks and intervenes in ways designed to push them gently along toward the general goals which have been established. The tasks are defined in what could be called 'process terms' because they ask children to investigate, to observe, to paint, to write; the children then interpret the tasks in terms of what they know they can do and carry them out in their individual ways and at a level appropriate for them. The teacher influences their growth through the judicious prompting of self-evaluation strategies, comments on how their efforts impress him and suggestions for improvement. The teacher thus assertively expects children to grow by providing the necessary support and direction, yet within a non-pressurized setting.

Such a role is demanding because it requires considerable deliberateness and analysis at each point when talking with a child. There must be a careful balance between giving children the direction necessary for them to grow in their abilities to communicate, to make decisions and to solve problems on the one hand and, on the other, telling them what to do specifically. Focusing children's attention on one point in the development of a certain process, for example, does much to achieve this balance, but this requires that the teacher understands thoroughly the nature of the process involved and the stages through which one moves as one grows in it. The teacher sees the continuity of growth, the point at which children may be and the way in which children may be encouraged to move forward; the objective for the teacher then becomes a matter of directing them only as much as is necessary to nudge them along, with the quality and character of the activity still largely determined by the children.

As so often observed before, this class uses the basic skills in the context of pursuing other ends. Language work is practiced and thereby developed as children write up the results of their scientific investigations and as they attempt to respond to music through storywriting. Mathematics, too, becomes yet another way of communicating information collected during their scientific study. Thus, while these children work on certain language and mathematics skills in isolation from time to time, the majority of their experience is spent using them in other academic pursuits and thereby honing and refining them.

Later that week, during the regular assembly, several of the children share their accomplishments from these activities with the entire school. They demonstrate how they categorized different sounds made when objects were struck, explain how a drum produces sound, share lists of words which describe sounds and read sections of their stories. As they make their presentations, the headteacher asks them questions about their work — how they organized themselves, what steps they followed, what they thought was the most exciting or most difficult part of their experience.

This event underlines key characteristics of the organic curriculum. The school sees the sharing process as a responsibility within a learning cycle; children learn much from their peers as they listen to the content of their talk, to the description of how they worked and to the excitement accompanying their presentations. The presenters also acquire a sense of accomplishment and a feeling of closure. Quite clearly the head is stressing the importance of processes in learning when he encourages reflection on how people work. He also recognizes the powerful role of affective forces in learning which at times excite and at other times challenge and even frustrate. Focusing on all of these dimensions in the assembly setting makes the goals of the school clear to all and supports the efforts of teachers and children toward those goals.

Children of Eleven and Twelve Years

A view of the eldest children in this particular school complements the previous observations and analyses of the eight and nine-year-olds who are just beginning their experience here and the ten and eleven-year-olds who are well underway. Teachers at all levels value the elements in the organic curriculum and the development of solid relationships among all members of the school community. Continuity is crucial if broad educational goals are to be achieved. At this fourth-year stage the efforts of the staff as a whole are likely to come to fruition.

During the morning session, the children are working on their proposed plans for their private rooms at home, an activity set for them the previous day. While they acknowledge that the task is hypothetical at least for the present time, they attack it with enthusiasm. They exchange ideas with each other and consult books and magazines which describe methods of remodeling, furniture and room arrangements for homes. As the children design their personal environment for both work and leisure, they make scale drawings of the room's dimensions and the position and size of furniture in the room, illustrate how the room would look and write accompanying descriptions.

The teacher provides direction and feedback as necessary. He asks one boy to examine his pencil drawing next to the written description to consider whether it would be clear to someone from outside the class who might look at it. 'Are the labels as clear as they need to be? Is the drawing as clear as it needs to be? I'm not saying that it isn't finished. I'm just asking you to look at it and check it.' With another child who is writing about her room, the teacher comments, 'It is your own work, so only you know if it is right'.

Here again the children bring together skills and concepts reflective of several content areas in the curriculum. Mathematics skills, applied while drawing rooms and furniture to a selected scale, are connected to the overall task of designing a den which will fit into a particular space in a home. Writing skills are also critical in the process of clearly communicating what kind of environment the children desire. The designs also incorporate children's sense of what is aesthetically pleasing to them.

Even with these eleven-year-olds, first-hand experience plays an important role in their work. Proceeding from their direct knowledge of the space they study and relax in at home, they move to locating information in resource materials found in everyday life. In both respects they are using their experience to direct their more academic efforts.

It is also apparent that such recognition of the value of out-of-school life can heighten the children's interest in the task at hand and can thus contribute to a child-centred atmosphere. School work may begin to make sense to children, at least with regard to some of their activities. Moreover, the development of these plans provides opportunities for the teacher and children to nurture their interpersonal relationships and in turn establish a firm basis for future interaction. The teacher may see another side of a child, respond personally as a caring adult and thereby make real the school's concern for the development of the 'whole child'.

A process orientation permeates this pattern of work. The task of applying basic skills to the solution of a general problem set by the teacher leads children to many possibilities, depending on their interests, specific talents and competence. What links together these variations, however, is the intention that children should practice basic mathematics and language skills in relevant contexts and continue refining their process skills — abilities to communicate clearly, to organize their thinking, to locate and analyze information and so on. The children must also examine their own efforts and decide how they should proceed depending on their evaluations. The processes of reflection and self-evaluation are thus valued as well. Such emphases will serve children well in future endeavours where these abilities might be required.

Later in the morning the teacher structures a movement lesson for the children. After changing into appropriate attire, the class files into the school's hall or assembly room. The teacher talks with the children about what a twist is and what movements are involved. As the teacher gives them verbal instructions, the children experiment with twisting their bodies in as many ways as possible. 'Find as many movements with twists in them as you can. Use twists that your body can comfortably make.' The children work with great concentration while the teacher gives further direction to shape their efforts: 'It is not essential to turn around completely each time, nor must you turn in the same direction each time'. Individual movements are carefully practiced. The teacher then instructs them to 'make a pattern with three to five twists in it'. The children try different combinations. As they put their ideas together into a sequence, the teacher directs them to 'finish it through to the end, to end it and hold it there for a moment'. He comments on their work by cautioning a child to 'keep it clear' or by suggesting that a boy 'move out of one twist and into another and out of that and into another'. The lesson concludes with a different exercise during which the children move freely and rapidly around the room while the teacher dramatically taps a cymbal in different sound patterns.

During this session integration of curriculum content areas is less obvious than in other examples of organic teaching. However, other elements of the organic curriculum play a significant part. A process orientation seems primary as the children work to develop their skills in using their bodies flexibly. Direct experience is of course inherent in the instruction. Child-centredness, too, is fundamental because the children focus on developing their psychomotor skills in reference to their own capabilities rather than in competition with others. The children are also able to vary their behaviours to reflect individual preferences. Further, the very focus upon movement skills indicates the commitment of the organic curriculum to the development of the wide range of human abilities in all individuals throughout their primary education. The body is clearly as important as the mind.

The teacher's instruction in this example also deserves comment. He adopts a verbal approach to give the children firm direction, but without restricting their decisions which might have happened if he had demonstrated and they had imitated. The analytical style is consistent with the overall concern of the school to develop competent and reflective learners. Certainly, too, there is a cross-over from this type of verbal instruction to language work in other parts of the curriculum.

After the midday break the class constructs various cuboids. They are following printed directions in order to assemble examples of three-dimensional objects which they will be studying in greater detail. Some children work individually, while others form pairs. Finished constructions are hung from the ceiling. The teacher not only helps the children carry out the immediate task but also stresses concepts related to two-dimensional and three-dimensional mathematical problems.

This simple activity makes several important statements about the organic curriculum. Even with this age group working on advanced material, the teacher begins with concrete, manipulative experiences. Principles of human development indicate that first-hand experience is the most effective starting point for later abstract work. Here, too, is an emphasis on basic skills, this time in relative isolation from other curriculum areas. However, there is the presumption that after the children achieve a certain competency, they will apply their skills in situations which may arise within other content areas or as they solve problems which reflect concerns from many of the traditional disciplines. The children also see the connections between the tools for learning, which they have just constructed, and what they are learning.

In addition, the activity provides an opportunity in which the children can develop their working and social relationships with each other. Focus on carrying out pre-stated instructions helps them cooperate and at times divide labour. The teacher's interactions with children in this unstressful setting can also be relaxed, helping to achieve those quality personal relationships so central to the organic curriculum.

The end of the school day demonstrates a similar concern. For the last fifteen minutes the teacher continues to read a short novel to the group. These quiet moments close the day on a relaxed and intimate note. The content of the story, if well chosen, may also provide a forum for discussing complex issues faced by early adolescents, for considering ways of making decisions and for appreciating other points of view. The storytime, valued even for these upper primary children, thus integrates the many goals of the organic curriculum, both intellectual and personal.

Discussion of Underlying Themes

These vignettes may be familiar to many who work in certain types of schools. To others, however, these views of the organic curriculum in action may present an approach to providing for the education of children seven-to-twelve which differs markedly from their experience. The purpose of this chapter has been to offer both groups examples of organic teaching drawn from actual school situations along with analysis of the underlying dynamics. The cumulative effect of such examples is to suggest the nature of the organic curriculum without oversimplifying it or reducing it to a set of practices for imitation by others. They give the necessary flesh to the elemental characteristics discussed in preceding chapters.

Several themes have been apparent throughout these examples. The four elements of the organic curriculum are clearly demonstrated. Child-centredness influences the way in which teachers shape their decisions, as well as the nature of their interactions in the classrooms. While the interests of the children are more important in determining the direction of activities, teachers take these interests and use them to accomplish goals deemed necessary in order for children to grow and function in society. The progressive development of concepts, processes and language and mathematical skills is thereby intertwined with the acknowledgement of children's interests and previous experiences.

Child-centredness naturally leads to a recognition of the need for an experiential base to learning. Focusing on children and observing their learning closely provide the data for viewing the provision of first-hand experience as a necessary component of teaching children aged seven to twelve. Similarly, the integration of the traditional curriculum areas seems to occur quite easily and spontaneously when responding to the learning patterns of children. The experience base appropriate for children is seldom neatly categorizable into one or another academic discipline, and hence, the resulting learning activities will likely contain a mix of content areas. This is not to say, of course, that the curriculum goals cannot be stated in terms of various specific content areas or even that some goals cannot be addressed separately from time to time. Rather, the way in which these goals are addressed often reflects a need for an interaction among the standard ways of knowing if children are to be able to learn in keeping with their stages of cognitive growth and the nature of their interests.

Because such interaction among content areas occurs principally during children's activities growing out of first-hand experiences, there seems to be a strong applicative bent to their work in the classroom. Through their efforts they see, hear, feel and touch how ideas demonstrate themselves in typical situations and thereby gain increased understanding of the ideas themselves and of their potential use in a variety of human activity. The process orientation of the curriculum also becomes central. To the extent that skills in language and mathematics are employed in order to solve problems and communicate results, these basic processes are further developed. Other process skills receive attention since they are called upon in the course of carrying out learning activities; it is here that they gain their meaning for children and are practiced and therefore refined for appropriate application in subsequent situations. The process orientation of the organic curriculum thus follows from its concern for incorporating first-hand experience and acknowledging the appropriateness of frequently integrating the content areas.

Thus far this summary has reiterated how the four elements of the organic curriculum have operated within the examples of teachers and children working in various learning situations. More than one element is clearly evident at any given moment, with each subsequently supporting the other in order to facilitate children's learning. The interaction of the elements appears as synergistic and almost inevitable. In addition, the more they function together in learning activities, the more they are likely to do so in future work; a momentum develops which lends a certain character to learning.

The relationships among teachers and children are critical in the organic curriculum because they establish the framework within which learning may take place. While the environment is child-centred, the role of adult authority is clear. Teachers are charged with helping children develop certain knowledges, understandings and skills deemed necessary by society, and they take this responsibility seriously. Within the context of firmly acknowledging the necessity of certain work, teachers respect the personhood of children and thereby model patterns of social behaviour important for them to acquire. Teachers also get to know children as individuals and, to the extent that is appropriate, recognize their interests and concerns in the definition of work the classes undertake; quite likely, this differentiation will occur in the provision of options to develop core learnings, in adaptations of the class environment and in tailoring teacher assistance to fit children's personalities and levels of accomplishment.

The quality of relationships among teachers and children both determine how the norms of acceptable behaviour will be maintained and influence the future nature of those relationships. Because the organic curriculum recognizes that personal interactions are important avenues for social learning, the way in which a teacher responds to inappropriate behaviour becomes a teaching method in itself. There then might be extensive discussion with the child to explore the options available and the consequences of each, the responsibility people have for their own decisions and the behaviour resulting from them and the need for all to be accountable for commitments made.

Teachers also make it clear that they are responsible for ensuring that the rights of all in a group are respected. In no small way the cumulative effect becomes one of promoting a democratic environment where each individual has both rights and responsibilities and where the interests of the individual cannot be pursued at the expense of other individuals. In this sense the teacher directly influences children's understanding of their relationships with others and the role of groups in our modern societies.

The organic curriculum also develops the relationships of children to materials and tools. Children learn how to use certain materials and tools in more controlled settings so that later they are able to select them appropriately when presented with new learning tasks. They learn the potential use of materials and tools by actually using them in their work and recognize their character and limits through directed experimentation and investigation. If our society truly requires of people effective problem-solving more than rote knowledge or imitative practice, then people who have developed a sense of what can and cannot be done with particular materials and tools will be in a better position to approach such problems confidently, creatively and knowledgeably.

These themes characterize the organic curriculum in action. The concerns to which they respond are pervasive throughout the decision-making of teachers even though at a particular moment these themes may not all be present. It must be remembered, too, that the implementation of the organic curriculum always employs a unique artistry in response to the complex challenges of nurturing the growth of a group of individual children.

Finally, it is important to recognize that the process of discussing these scenarios primarily offers a way of observing and interpreting what goes on during organic teaching. Teachers in other settings may proceed in a similar fashion when clarifying their experience. A close examination of school life and a reflection upon the meaning of events for all participants can lead to a more enlightened approach to helping our children learn.

Chapter 5

Creating A Climate For Learning

In previous chapters the emphasis has been on the interaction between the teacher and the child in fulfilment of the organic curriculum. This chapter and the next one examine ways of moving towards that fulfilment. They suggest ways of structuring and facilitating children's learning experiences at class and school level over a period of time. It begins by identifying some of the underlying principles which inform the actions of the teacher at the classroom level.

Schools, like other institutions within society, are subject to public scrutiny and the general pressures which are exerted through, for example, newspapers, television and politicians. Often education is spoken of in general terms with references to standards and achievements, attitudes and behaviour. Individual schools develop reputations as 'good' or 'bad' schools or become known because of their language work, their science work, or their art work. These reputations are conferred by professionals, such as other teachers and inspectors, or lay people, such as parents and the general community. A whole school is referred to as an entity with the suggestion that all individuals within it match those general characteristics used to describe the institute. Internally, primary schools are organized to deal with groups of children. The headteacher or principal is responsible for the whole school and the whole staff. Each teacher is responsible for a class. Within the class there may be other sub-groups, changing from hour to hour, day to day, or week to week.

Within and around this reality there is a constant demand that the teachers remain aware of the needs of individual children and continually recognize and react to the individual differences that exist among them. The general pressures which surround the operation of educational institutions mean that they must constantly remind themselves of this truth.

First-Hand Experience

A phrase which is often used in talking about primary education is 'first-hand experience'. It is used to encompass a wide variety of activities which children pursue in school. While there may be disagreement as to what does and does not fit into that category, it is generally recognized that first-hand experience is important in the development of everyone, whether children or adults. The earlier discussion in Chapters 2 and 3 explores some of the theory relating to experience based-learning.

Experiences relate to each other. In order to make sense of a new experience we each have to call on our previous experiences. Furthermore, everyone has a unique set of experiences to draw upon.

A group of teachers on an introductory weekend at an outdoor education centre were taken to visit a show cave which their children would be visiting at a future date. The teachers came from ten different education authorities and some twenty or so different schools. They taught children between the ages of seven and twelve. There were men and women between the ages of twenty-three and fifty-five, a group of about thirty-five people. For some of them it was the first residential visit they were planning for their children. For others, such visits were an annual event. Some were experienced in taking children into the countryside and walking in the hills. Two were experienced potholers and cavers. For a few more, it was to be the first time they had ever entered a cave. As they approached the cave mouth, the variety of comments illustrated the different emotions that the group were feeling. The fears, the bravado, the confidence, the ignorance and the knowledge were all there to be heard, almost to be felt. When the group went into the cave, they each took with them their own previous experience alongside their current awareness. As the teachers entered the first gallery, full of stalagmites and stalactites, with pools of light and deep patches of darkness, they each made comparisons, comparisons with other caves of which they were aware. Perhaps they had visited them, perhaps they had seen them on television or read about them in a book. Each person was drawing on different experiences and the differing contexts of those experiences. Then they were fitting this current and new experience alongside those other recollections. Even for the guide, who came into this cave four or five times a day, this was a new experience. The cave was the same, but the people were different and the time was different. The only experience each member of the group had shared was this visit, to this cave, on this occasion. They each brought to the experience a different set of constructs, concepts and awareness. From combining these with the current experience they each created their own reality.

From all this awareness we must select, and what we select and call consciousness is never the same as awareness because the process of selection mutates it. We take a handful of sand from the endless landscape of awareness around us and call the handful of sand the world. (Pirsig, 1976, p. 75)

It is the same when we offer a group of children an experience. It becomes a part of their awareness. They have experienced it. Each selects from it, interprets it differently and combines it with previous consciousness. They differ in the way that their consciousness develops but they all have had a shared experience.

The way the teacher selects experiences and activities and presents displays and materials affects the degree of involvement and commitment which the children make. The acceptance of the individual nature of responses to those stimuli has to be returned to again and again when considering the relevance of first-hand experience to children's learning since, as has already been stated, schools are organized to support group rather than individual activity.

The Teacher as Curriculum Planner

Children learn best when new experiences are related to what they already know, when they are novel but not too strange and when they are sufficiently complex to call for some extension of ideas but are not outside the range of understanding. The associated Piagetian theory has already been discussed in Chapter 2. To provide such experiences on every occasion for each individual in a class is impossible. With appropriate planning we can increase the level of match between the experience and the previous awareness of the child. By doing this we can increase the degree of involvement for individual children and for the group.

However it is important that planning is at an appropriate level. Sometimes it can be very rigid and demand such conformity as to be a straightjacket which allows no freedom of movement or initiative by any of the participants in the learning process. A head or a teacher will plan a topic, or several topics, in the finest detail, which the class will follow with no deviation from the original blueprint. Some schools have a system which covers the whole school, so that children entering the school in the first year follow a preplanned range of topic work through to the time they leave. Each year group may have six topics which they have to cover. For example the first year may begin in September with Ponds and, in November, continue with Railways. After Christmas, in the new term, the areas of study may be

Night and Space, followed by Pets. In the final term the topics are Ourselves and Farms. The other year groups have similar lists so that after four years each child has 'done' twenty-four topics. The pattern is the same year after year, with the topics fixed.

To ensure that the system works, the teaching staff spend many hours preparing flow charts and work cards in a tightly constructed web of theoretical relationships with cross references not only to other work cards and flow charts but also to other available resources. Within the school there are support materials including reference books, slides and computer software. There is a collection of ten to eleven thousand prepared workcards relating to the different topics and judged to be aimed at different ability levels. It is not anticipated that teachers or children will deviate from this detailed plan. Should something of interest occur outside the title under consideration it will be ignored. Should something of significance occur within the local environment relating to the topic but not covered in the plan, it may be assimilated into the class work providing it does not prevent the planned work being done. There is no room for opportunism, there is no room for the unexpected, there is no room for individuality.

This is very conscientious planning with a high degree of commitment from the teachers, and many hours of hard work in preparation, but it is planning which denies the very essence of learning. It is a closed, tight structure which directs children into many hours of activity. Unfortunately the activity is seldom related to the child's experience, is second rate and second-hand. It keeps children occupied. Within the classroom the teachers have very few decisions to make regarding the intellectual and affective development of the children in their care. They know which card the child will move on to, and they know what the outcomes from each card will be, whether writing, science, mathematics or art. The results are as pre-determined as the activities. It is this image of planning, of structure, which is the very antithesis of what planning for learning should be.

In the primary classroom teachers are responsible for the education of their children for the year they have them in their charge. With the aid of colleagues, they have to try and accommodate the needs of their children in a wide variety of areas of experience. They have to involve them in the aesthetic and expressive areas such as art, movement, music, writing and drama. They have to help them explore the world in which they live through science, history, geography and mathematics. At the same time they have to help their children become more aware of the social dimensions and obligations which are expected of them.

Every topic or area of study which is explored by a class cannot include all of these areas of experience except by the creation of tortuous connections which do not really exist. Some selection by the teacher has to be made, a conscious selection where the teacher is not only aware of which areas will provide the focus for a particular study but also aware of those which are to be excluded. Thus any omission is by design rather than default.

It is possible to see the planning of topic work fitting into four broad stages:

Examining the possible;
Identifying the probable;
Action and activities;
Further developments.

Examining the Possible

The first is an examination of the possible, a broad overview of all the areas a topic may include. In a sense it is a preplanning stage, when the mind can roam widely over an extensive range of possibilities. It may take the form of a flow chart or a diagram or an abundance of notes. If it is concerned with 'Fire' it may begin with the efforts of prehistoric man, touch on events such as the Great Fire of London and include a visit to the local fire station. Indeed it may include every pyrotechnic event from the creation of the world to the Day of Judgment. Similarly, possibilities for specific activities in which the children may become involved can be very wide reaching.

Identifying the Probable

The teacher is operating within certain constraints which affect this initial thinking, for example the availability of material, the previous experience of the children, time and the expectations of the school. Soon that examination of the possible becomes more realistic. In this second stage the teacher focuses on the probable range of experiences and activities. They are more precisely identified and the practical problems of providing such activities are taken into account. The various constraints mentioned, together with other considerations, influence the selection. Eventually, an overall plan emerges which provides a realistic basis for action.

Action and Activities

Often the focus for the topic work is centred on a major experience. The third stage in planning is closely allied to this focus. The experience varies according to the nature of the topic to be studied. It may be a half day or day visit to an appropriate venue. Sometimes it is a series of activities or experiences within the school. On at least one occasion during the child's time at the school, it is related to a residential field visit involving several nights away from home. Having decided what that central and important activity is, the teacher analyzes it more closely. The introductory work in school prior to the visit has to be appropriate in focusing the children's thinking towards the particular event. Any necessary skills or concepts or information which the children will require to maximize the experience will be introduced using a variety of pedagogical styles.

If this major input is a visit, it involves at least two teachers with a class of children together with other adults such as parents and non-teaching assistants. This requires planning and coordination with colleagues. What actually occurs on the visit varies with the venue chosen. Some situations offer greater opportunity for involvement and doing than others. Sometimes there is an opportunity to question significant adults who work, for example, at the fire station or railway station. In other situations, such as a visit to an industrial museum there is an opportunity for improvized drama. Whatever else happens, there is always some very careful looking and discussion and, whenever possible, some drawing and note-taking. These activities develop the children's looking and generate more tightly framed questions and discussion. On return to school they provide a reminder of the shared experiences and help in channelling and supporting follow-up work.

Planning the introduction to the topic and the experience or visit itself also includes planning for the work which will arise out of them. This is particularly important when it is realized that a single day visit may provide the major stimulus for anything from four to eight weeks' work. Although some possibilities only present themselves after a particular event has occurred, the teacher can anticipate most avenues of enquiry and prepare accordingly. There are many questions to be answered in order to make such preparation:

> Will all of the children work on the same idea at the same time or will there be opportunities for group and individual work?
> Will there be a wide or narrow range of materials available for work in, say, art or writing?
> Will children have a large degree of freedom in organizing their work space, their colleagues and their work?
> How far will these be prescribed by the teacher?
> To what degree will this vary for individual children?
> What percentage of each week's work will be spent on this particular area of study?

For how many weeks is it envisaged that such work will continue?

Even at this stage the way in which individual teachers frame and answer questions highlights their sensitivity and flexibility which in turn can enhance or subdue the quality of the child's response.

Further Developments

The final stage in planning is when the teacher looks further ahead and tries to consider how the topic may develop, for example, what other activities, materials and experiences can be introduced to enhance, deepen or redirect the way in which the work is moving. The nature of these developments is variable but may include a further visit, the sharing of a video film or a story, or the opportunity to carry out additional activities or experiments. Thus the major initial impetus is extended and the focus, even if slightly changed in its direction, is kept sharp. At this time, all of these questions, possibilities and practicalities, can be answered to a certain degree but the teacher is aware that situations may, indeed will, change when the work gets under way.

As the work begins, certain assumptions about the children's level of understanding and development may be incorrect. The response of the children to the visit or activity may have a different emphasis from that envisaged. The work may take longer than expected, or the children may move very quickly in their learning and execution of ideas. The involvement of the children in a particular aspect of the work may mean a deepening of the investigation. In turn this may mean that a narrower range of work will be covered. No matter how thoughtful the planning has been, from those first initial explorations of the many possibilities through to the execution of the realities, the teacher has to be ready to accommodate and assimilate changing circumstances and to retain flexibility in order to maximize the learning process. Every outcome cannot be forecast and planned for. If the approach which has been outlined is followed it may increase the chances of involving the teacher and the child in a partnership for learning which can grow and develop with the needs of the learner.

Partnership with Colleagues

At each of the four stages of planning discussed above the teacher will be looking at possibilities in a variety of curriculum areas. Decisions are made about appropriate resources, material, content and pedagogy. While every topic will not include every curriculum area, all topics will include several areas from the wide range of activities which occur in the primary school. Yet while the teacher is responsible for all of the work children do across the whole curriculum range, it is not realistic to expect expertise in every field.

At all stages of planning, teachers operate as members of a team. It is important for teachers to be free to call on colleagues with expertise in areas complementary to their own. Within the school each staff member, including the head, has specific curriculum responsibilities. These responsibilities commit teachers to take the initiative in promoting and discussing their particular fields. In terms of curriculum planning this means discussing possibilities, probabilities and extensions of work with colleagues whenever possible.

There is, then, a two-way expectation. Class teachers are expected to approach colleagues with a curriculum responsibility in areas different from their own to ask for advice and support, and the curriculum responsibility holders are expected to approach the class teachers, to offer advice and support in the planning and execution of work at class level. For the curriculum responsibility holder this may mean working with a colleague in the classroom, or suggesting sources of ideas, or providing support materials. However it is important to remember that class teachers have both roles to play since they have a class and a curriculum responsibility.

In many schools it is possible for the head to be involved from the beginning in supporting the plans of a class teacher. It is the norm that from the very early stages headteachers will be involved in ongoing informal discussion. Headteachers have an overview of the total school situation. They are aware of when other teachers have used similar starting points and can help the class teacher to avoid problems which other teachers may have met on previous occasions. They can facilitate the practical issues concerning arrangements for visits or identifying and obtaining resources. They can direct teachers to certain colleagues who will share their experiences and knowledge about the occasions when they have been involved with children in similar areas of investigation and activity. They can also remind the teacher of which colleagues have particular curriculum knowledge or who may be able to offer ideas. These clearly defined support strategies are important but they are not all used on every occasion. The discussions between head and the class teacher indicate which action may be appropriate at that time. In addition heads have certain personal strengths relating to curriculum and organization and can contribute to the teacher's thinking and planning. However the central importance of the head's role at this time is the maintenance of a working relationship with the class teacher. It is important that the teacher knows the head is interested in what is happening in the classroom, is prepared to support what the teacher wishes to do, and is available with constructive criticism and practical help should they be necessary. While such direct and ongoing communication may be more difficult in a larger school, it is still necessary to identify a significant senior colleague within the school system who can support the class teacher in a similar way to that outlined above.

The Teacher and the Child

In spite of the support which a teacher may receive from others in the school, in the final analysis it is the responsibility of the class teacher to put the planning into operation. It is the class teacher, regardless of particular curriculum strengths and weaknesses, who must instigate, support and coordinate the work of the children. Whatever the area of study the teacher will encourage such attitudes as initiative, perseverance, care and self-reliance. These attitudes and associated skills will apply across the whole curriculum and if they are to flourish the teacher must create an appropriate relationship with the children.

The many hours spent by the teacher in providing an interesting environment, preparing visits, making checklists and curriculum plans, and consulting with colleagues will have relevance and promote learning only if the personal relationship between teacher and child is mutually encouraging. A significant factor in developing that relationship is the teacher's sincere and continual recognition of the worthwhile contribution that every child makes to the class. The approach is one of building on success and self-worth while making comments of a sufficiently rigorous nature to extend thinking and self-awareness. This is a very difficult path to tread but its importance cannot be over-emphasized. The significance for learning is that it begins to free children to make honest statements about themselves and to become more aware of who they are.

It is only within a trusting relationship that children will begin to give of themselves. In this piece of writing, Carol, who is 11, shared a secret from her past and her feelings are very clear.

'I was only little and I had a gerbil, two to be exact but one was my sister's. I was playing in the bathroom letting them run about, when one got out of the door. It ran into my sister's bedroom and under the bed. I tried to catch it and it took me quite some time before I did. I was really mad and as a punishment I gave it a hard squeeze. I put it down again and it would not go. I pushed it, shook it, and I realized I had killed it. I took them both downstairs and put them away. I said nothing to no one. That night some neighbours came round and my dad whistled the gerbils to come out of their little hut. One appeared so my dad got the other one out of the hut. 'It's dead', he said. I went white, said nothing, but my heart was in my mouth. He never found out until a few years back when I got hold of a gerbil by its tail and part of its fur came off. I hid it but was found out. I was so upset I confessed to everything.

While Carol was aware that her writing would be read by her teacher, she also knew that it would only be shared with other children in the class or a wider audience if she gave her permission because the teacher had made that contract with her.

Another example demonstrates that the development of mutual trust between the child and the teacher is not only to enable the child to explore herself, but also to encourage a sensitive awareness of the people with whom she comes into contact. When Elaine was asked to write about someone she knew she wrote this about another teacher in the school.

Mr Phillips

Mr Phillips is the headmaster of my school which is Jackson Primary School.
He takes half of our class for maths. I am in his maths group.
He always makes us laugh because he says that he is a handsome, beautiful, intelligent man but we just say you must be joking.
I know I shouldn't say this but I noticed that Mr Phillips is going bald at the top of his head.
Mr Phillips has brown hair and a browny ginger beard.

There are several elements of this writing which are significant. It is not particularly long or verbose. It is honest, perceptive, slightly humorous and polite. Most significantly, the child felt free to say it. She felt secure in her relationship with her teacher to commit her ideas to public scrutiny. It is this relationship which is at the heart of the learning process. The catalyst between the experience and the child that causes learning and growth is the quality of the human interaction between the child and the teacher.

Sir Alec Clegg, the last Chief Education Officer for the West Riding of Yorkshire, referred to the difference between mind and spirit:

In the school and the classroom the difference between mind and spirit shows itself in simpler ways which are within our grasp. There is for instance the difference between the mechanical process of reading and the enjoyment of what is read; between the mechanics of musical notation and sensitive playing and singing; between writing on a prescribed topic from notes on the blackboard and telling someone in your own personal written words of something that has excited you; between lessons on perspective and giving the child the urge to draw or model or paint what he sees in his way; between the child who is made to do the Tudors or do the Stuarts or start with the Ancient Britons in the hope of one day arriving at Elizabeth I and the child whose interest is aroused by how his grandfather and his grandmother lived when they were young or by the origins of the local railway or canal or factory . . . between the teacher whose subject is adjusted to his own ability and the child's needs and the teacher who merely follows the syllabus . . . between the head of a school who sees the timetable and framing and observation of school rules as his main task and one who, by the use of recognition, expectation and encouragement, draws the best out of colleagues and pupils. (Clegg, 1972, p. 10)

There are times when instruction, information, skills and timetabling are necessary but they only have meaning if they enhance the understanding of the recipients. For this to happen an awareness of children as people with unique personal and intellectual needs, an awareness of the spirit as well as of the mind, has to be present in the teacher. Then children are more prepared to make honest statements about their perceptions of the world. As children use not only writing, but also art materials, drama, movement, scientific analysis and mathematical formulae, to explain where their understanding is, the teacher becomes more informed as to what activity or investigation will provide the next appropriate experience and develops a clearer idea of where they might move to next.

While the organization of the primary school means that the most significant relationship is between the class teachers and the children in the classes, this alone is not sufficient. There are times when a teacher has to meet with other children, for example at breaks when supervising the playground, in taking assemblies or in specialist teaching situations. The movement of people about the school means that there is a constant opportunity for teachers to show their interest in children not in their immediate care. During school session there will be times when a teacher is in the immediate vicinity of children from another class engaged in a task. The teacher can respond positively to the work being done, offer encouragement and, if appropriate, engage the children in conversation. The constant transmission by the staff of a care and concern for all of the children they meet helps to maintain a feeling of individual worth.

Within most schools there are statements of intent which explore and emphasize some of the issues under discussion as well as outline various curriculum expectations. These can provide a framework for what the school does. A comparison of written statements of intent shows great similarity from one school to the next. However, a visit to several schools soon shows the divergence in practices and attitudes. It is what actually happens that is more significant than what is written down. The school as a whole must accept the importance of all personal relationships through action as well as through rhetoric. If such relationships are a reality rather than an intention, there is some chance of the organic, changing, curriculum meeting the needs of the children.

A high quality of interaction between the teacher and the child is essential in creating an appropriate climate for learning but part of that climate is determined by the organization and presentation of materials and resources. Any discussion of classroom organization and practices can only occur within the context of the acknowledgement of the importance of this relationship.

Organizing for Learning

The Use of Space

Any school building will have its own particular characteristics depending on its age, architecture and state of repair. The variety of teaching spaces available range from the isolated, box-like, classroom through to the open plan school whose work areas are only determined by the movable furnishings and fittings. These aspects of schools are not in the control of the teacher.

Within those constraints, even in the most traditional of buildings, it is still possible for the teaching staff to influence the organization of teaching space. It is the teacher who can identify the appropriate spaces which are necessary for certain activities to take place. Some attempts can be made to create work areas which match the identified needs of the children. It is not possible to guarantee what particular activity will be seen on walking into a school involved with an organic approach to learning. Within the rhythm of the school day there are a variety of activities occurring.

Some of the work is active and practical. Domestic science requires certain items of equipment, workspace and facilities for cooking and baking. It is easier to keep this as a specialist area although any teacher may work there with a group of children. Similarly areas for certain art activities are more easily maintained and controlled by keeping them permanently set up.

Of course other curriculum areas require children to move about and do things. For example, science work at the primary level does not demand a special science laboratory, but it does mean that children need to be able to organize themselves, find any necessary materials or equipment to help their enquiries, and then find a suitable space in which to work. The space needs to be organized to facilitate this process. Art will mean space for easels, the storage of unfinished and finished work, the availability of materials and a variety of different sized work stations. This also requires forethought and flexibility. Certainly for physical education and possibly for music there is a room set aside in which a class or a group may work.

In contrast there is a need for spaces where more passive work can occur. There will be times when quiet, clean work has to be pursued without undue visual and aural interference. Such work includes reading and writing, the use of reference books and the development of number skills as well as the recording of more active work experiences in curriculum areas such as science and social studies.

Sometimes only one or two children will be involved in an activity. At other times there may be six or seven children. Occasions also occur when the class comes together to listen to the teacher, to share poetry and literature and to share work and progress with each other.

Just as the nature of the activity and the size of group vary, so does the role of the teacher. At times, the activity demands that the role be didactic and directing. A different task requires more openness and informality. During a working day the teacher calls on a variety of approaches along a wide spectrum, thereby matching teaching style to the needs of the children.

The need for flexibility in the use of space is underlined as each of these variables, activity, group size and teaching style, change over time. During any one day there is often a multiple use of a given space. A set of tables is used for writing, number work, drawing and reading within a few hours. Other spaces may have only a single use. The easel for painting is left set out for the child to return to although it has been moved to the side of the room to facilitate ease of movement for other children when it is not in use. An area close to the book shelves is set aside for quiet reading and reference work, and there are the practical areas described earlier.

In order to facilitate the appropriate use of space it is necessary for the teacher not only to consider the issues outlined above, but also to develop the children's ability to organize for themselves. Thus the children can arrange the work spaces for different activities as and when necessary with the minimum of interruption to the learning process. It is clearly established in the minds of the children which are permanently passive or quiet areas, and which are open to rapid change and flexibility. Similarly it is clear to the children when they may choose their working space and where the limits of that choice are. In this way the organization of space can begin to accommodate the learning needs of the children.

The Use of Displays

The way in which the school uses displays and childrens' work to enhance the quality of the surroundings and the richness of the learning opportunities is an important element in the way space is organized. Often such displays are concerned with natural objects such as flowers, shells, feathers and stones. They are concerned with nature as designer and with encouraging children to look more closely at the world in which they live. Complementary to the natural objects are items relating to the man-made world. A collection of used vehicle parts or domestic items may be grouped together, or items from a different country and different culture may be used to broaden the children's awareness. Sometimes the display is related to a particular part of the school year. At Harvest time the local farm may be able to lend a collection of implements and tools which are relevant. During the summer there may be displays relating to children's family holidays. It would be easy to extend this list since the range of possibilities for displays is very wide.

The size of the displays varies according to the decision of the teacher. Often they will take up a space in the classroom on a cupboard top of perhaps one metre by a half metre. At other times they may involve lifesize figures and take up a much larger space.

There are many sources of artefacts for use on these occasions. The school may build its own collection of smaller items. Initially this will be limited but it will grow into a wide range of shells, fossils, stones, feathers, wood, glass, domestic goods, vehicle parts, fabrics, dried flowers and grasses. In addition each year the school can purchase a small number of stuffed animals or birds together with fabric drapes and display items to set off the artefacts. Often friends of the school or local shops will donate items of interest. Before very long the problem will be one of storing the ever-growing collection and rejecting items which are no longer appropriate.

The school does not need to rely totally on its own endeavours. The local education authority may operate a loan service which will offer a wider range of objects relating to the whole school curriculum than any one school can build up itself. Local museums may also make loans of items they have in storage. A final source of materials is the arrangement of informal exchanges with other schools in a similar situation serving whatever age range they may serve. This not only provides additional resources but also helps to develop good relationships between the schools involved.

Displays such as these act as a stimulus to learning in so many ways. The children are encouraged to handle and touch, to be actively curious, as well as just to look. The displays may act as a creator of atmosphere and ambience, as items to be specifically looked at and used, or as support to a visit; but essentially and most significantly they act as a generator of language, as a promoter of ideas and discussions.

Different, but just as important is the displaying of children's completed work. This practice underlines each child's achievements and allows for increased positive recognition by teacher and peers. There are various processes and factors influencing the selection of work for display. Finished items may be grouped to illustrate a particular theme or aspect of the work the class has been doing, such as responses to a visit to the local railway station. The work may also be of a similar form, for example, illustrated poems, paintings, or clay models. The teacher may display the work of a particular child to emphasize his or her specific achievement, or may focus on an area of the curriculum such as mathematics which may need general encouragement or emphasis.

In all cases children's work is presented carefully in order to reflect the importance the teacher gives to it. It then acts as a focus for discussion and the dissemination of ideas rather than just as 'wallpaper'. There is a benefit not only to the individual child whose work is on display but also to the whole of the class. In an open situation there is also a transfer of ideas to children and teachers in other classes which underlines the wholeness of the school's goals.

The Provision of Materials

An obvious but often overlooked element in creating the appropriate climate for the organic curriculum is the organization and presentation of materials and equipment. Some of these materials are expendable, such as paint, paper and pencils. Others are longer lasting and include easels, microscopes, measuring tools, as well as large equipment such as televisions and microcomputers. Because there are so many materials available and because it is clear that all are needed by every child, every class or even every school, the school needs to determine criteria for the selection of materials. Those criteria will be derived from the school's approach to children's learning. The sensitive selection of materials by the teacher is essential if children are to maximize the learning possibilities presented by the experiences they meet in school. The range of materials will affect the nature of the reaction the children can have to those experiences and thus their expression and development of ideas.

The importance of materials in their own right as a stimulus to thinking and learning cannot be ignored. The opportunity to handle clay, work with a computer, paint, use pen and ink, or build with technical materials, itself affects the child's development. For example, in attempting to solve a problem using a Logo-type computer program, Joanne created a new image on the screen through her command. This unintentional new image promoted a new train of thought. The original problem was filed away for future solution, and the new idea, stimulated by the response of the material, the Logo program, led the child into new areas of exploration.

On another occasion, John had been handling the pet hamster which is kept in the classroom. He had never handled a hamster before and all his senses were alive to the new situation; his eyes, ears, fingers and nose were interpreting the experience. His mind sorted and shaped the sensory responses and placed the experiences alongside related previous experiences like stroking the dog next door and the feel of his mother's fur coat. He decided to paint a picture of the hamster. After talking about it with the teacher and his friends he began modifying his ideas as he progressed. He tried to capture the smooth but furry appearance and the way the hamster clasped a sunflower seed in its front claws. A mark on the paper, made when he was trying to paint the straw, suggested another hamster. He added that. Then he painted the cage and the food dish and the drinking bottle. Many events changed his initial idea such as the recollection of other experiences and reflection on his recent experience. The marks made by the paint with the brush on the paper promoted other developments, new shapes, colours and textures being suggested by the material itself. Thus the experience of the materials extended his thinking and the expression of his experiences. The interaction between the child's experience and the attempt to express that experience is central in the process of individual growth. It is this inter-action which leads to a growth in understanding and awareness.

The provision of a definitive list of materials for each area of experience the school offers is not practical. Each school has to consider its own needs and develop a clear policy. All of the materials provided need to be of a high quality. A similarity of provision throughout the school for individual classrooms helps to promote a clarity of purpose. As a result, during their time in the school the children become familiar and confident with a manageable range of materials and equipment. The depth and quality of experience the children acquire enable them to use the materials to express with clarity and authority their reactions to and understanding of the world in which they live.

It is important that consideration be given to all of the school's work. In deciding for each curriculum area, it is necessary to continually question the appropriateness, necessity and quality of provision, always checking against whether it will help or hinder children's learning. For example, in writing, decisions are needed about the quality, size and colour of paper and about the type of pencil or pen to be used; in art, selection has to be made for drawing, painting, modelling, sewing and printing. Such selection of materials occurs with the other arts, in music, movement and drama. It extends to the scientific and mathematical areas of experience with the provision of appropriate structural apparatus, tools, and microscopes which extend the opportunities to compute, to measure and to observe. There is a need to make decisions about which computer programs are of value. Similar attention is given to the selection of reference books. They need to be regularly checked for suitability and difficulty. In addition other support materials such as maps, charts, slides, and films must be evaluated.

As well as deciding what materials will be provided, the school has to consider how available they will be to the children. Some of the materials that the school has decided to use will have to be controlled by the teacher but if a school is concerned with developing autonomy in learning, then some opportunity has to be made for children to make choices for themselves. The gradual development and extension of choices offered to children can lead to a parallel development and extension of response by the children to the experiences from which they are working. For this reason, the staff of the school need to constantly review the way in which the skill of choosing is developed and encouraged within the school.

In Summary

The degree to which learning is child-centred, integrated, experience-based and process-oriented is not solely determined by the class teacher. There are other factors affecting classroom practices. Nevertheless, the teacher has a degree of autonomy which has significant influence on the process of learning. This chapter has been concerned with planning and organization of the organic curriculum. In particular, the role of the teacher as curriculum planner, in partnership with colleagues, was examined at some length. In the context of the relationship between the teacher and the child, the organization of the classroom was seen as a central element in creating the appropriate conditions for learning to occur. The organization of space, the presentation of stimuli through displays and the selection of materials for children to use were examined as important parameters in determining the nature of the learning which takes place in the organic classroom.

Chapter 6

Classroom Practice and Evaluation

The creation of the appropriate climate for learning, in the ways outlined in the previous chapter, is an essential step in the development of the learning process. It provides a context within which children can participate in a variety of activities appropriate to their age and ability. The school has to provide these activities within an overall curriculum framework.

What Did You Do in School Today?

When children return home from school, they are often asked by their parents what they have been doing in school. In response children may offer an isolated incident, a particular activity, or simply reply that they have done nothing. Even an apparently full description of the day's activities will not encompass the total curriculum which the child will have experienced during the day.

> A school's curriculum consists of all those activities designed or encouraged within its organizational framework to promote the intellectual, personal, social and physical development of its pupils. It includes not only the formal programme of lessons, but also the 'informal' programme of so-called extra-curricular activities as well as all those features which produce the school's 'ethos', such as the quality of relationships, the concern for equality of opportunity, the values exemplified in the way the school sets about its task and the way in which it is organized and managed. (DES, 1985a, p. 7).

There have been innumerable analyses of both the informal and formal curriculum. An examination of the bibliography of Lawton (1975), or Alexander (1985) and others will provide substantial evidence to support this. For teachers in the classroom an awareness of current thinking regarding the curriculum is important in informing their actions. However, in an attempt to describe the complex network of interactions which occur in the school, certain elements may be isolated from the whole pattern. Such an analysis will often give only one perspective. It is not always the full picture. In the Schools Council Working Paper 75, *Primary Practice,* Chapter II is called 'Describing the Curriculum' and includes the following sections:

> *Describing the curriculum:*
>   The curriculum as subjects
>   Curriculum as process
>   Curriculum as the study of problems
>   Curriculum as areas of knowledge and experience
>   The curriculum through a child's eyes
>   (Schools Council Working Paper No. 75, 1982, p. 5)

Each of those five approaches to examining what we do in school has validity. They are not, however, mutually exclusive. On the contrary the curriculum, the organic curriculum, is a multifaceted, multilevel amalgam of process, subject, problem (or issue) and experience made available to the children. It is the balance between these different elements which will give a school its particular flavour when rhetoric is translated into practice. In the context of the climate for learning created by the school and the recognition of the complexity of the situation, it is possible to identify some of the elements which children meet.

In school children learn to read and write. They practice handwriting and regularly work at arithmetic. Sometimes the need for such basic skills will arise directly and obviously from the other work children are tackling. The school will have a list of objectives which, while remaining flexible to match the differing needs of individuals, will help the teachers in arriving at appropriate expectations of children's achievements.

Much of the work arises from the surrounding environment within which the children live and the range of experiences they meet. It may begin within the school, from artefacts brought into the school, or from people visiting the school. It may be concerned with the wider environment, for example, the school grounds, the surrounding streets, the local town, or, indeed, other regions of the country. It is concerned with finding out about the wider world in which each individual lives. Children find out about animals and their behaviour by keeping animals in school; they find out how people used to live by visiting historical houses and homes. They grow plants and explore the world of technology and science. Much of this finding out is supported by secondary sources of information, through books, computer software, and audio-visual materials. The children record what they discover in a variety of ways and ask more questions in a continuing cycle of exploration.

Parallel to finding out about other people and places, and about other times and technologies, children find out about themselves. There is a development of the affective aspects of children's growth. They use paint and clay and draw with pen and pencil. They use threads and fabrics and other materials to express ideas and images. They sing and make music and work at movement and drama. They use their bodies to express emotions and responses to their world. Part of the written work which is done is poetry and prose which gives opportunities for personal expression.

Other elements of a child's activities permeate the whole school experience. These activities are at the centre of the curriculum in that they are not the prerogative of any particular academic discipline. They apply across the curriculum.

There is a social code of expectation and socialization. This is part of the school 'ethos' referred to earlier in the DES statement. It includes learning about oneself and others and how, although we are all different individuals, there are certain common needs and similarities which help us to live alongside one another.

There is an emphasis on observation and on focusing down. This is obvious in areas such as drawing and painting. Teachers can be surprised at the clarity which children can bring to their work when they are encouraged to look carefully. Even here there will be a variety of expression from the scientific, accurate drawing of the ground beetle found outside the school, to the more interpretative painting of the tawny owl which had been brought into school. Each captures the essence of the subject but in very different ways; yet both are dependent on careful looking. Such a skill also has great relevance in handwriting, in reading and in spelling where the comparisons are often of a fine order and the degree of discrimination required is very high. Similarly in scientific experiments and in mathematical calculations, in map making and reference work, the same skills of observation are needed if children are to extend their understanding of the the world in which they live.

Part of the ethos of the school is the continual emphasis and encouragement to see a task through to a conclusion. This is not an acknowledgement of teacher pressure to finish the work, but of children taking on the notion for themselves. When a class is asked to write about an experience they have shared, the majority of the children may write two, three, or four pages. If a child has so much of value to say that it takes ten or twelve pages, the teacher has to encourage such a response and encourage such application and persistence. Similarly if children begin work and run into difficulties, it is important to help them overcome the difficulties and continue with their work rather than allow for an easy change of direction. The acceptance that different people need different lengths of time to complete a specific task and similarly that different tasks need different times allocated to them has implications for school organization.

It is important that children are given opportunities to make choices but children will only learn to choose when their experience is gradually enlarged. On the one hand they do not need too broad a choice for their level of experience. On the other hand they do not want to be offered such a limited choice that their decisions are meaningless.

Wise choosing is a skill which can be gradually encouraged and extended alongside the other challenges which children are offered in school. Whatever the age of the children, whatever the stimulus, whatever the intended response, they are encouraged to organize for themselves. The process involves decisions about where to work, what materials to use, what work to attempt and how long to work on it. Setting the parameters of those choices will be the responsibility of the teacher. Within those parameters the children and the teacher will discuss and negotiate the appropriate work structures. Over time the children's ability to make decisions will be extended and the parameters will be widened.

It is within the total context of the factors explored in this and the preceding chapter that the following three examples of organization for learning and the outcomes at class level can be examined and interpreted. If the factors which influence the learning process are as varied and as variable as has been suggested, it would be inappropriate to generalize from these descriptions. The intention is to exemplify many of the significant aspects of the learning process while avoiding the notion of a package of instant solutions which is directly transferable to any situation.

Growing Tomatoes

The starting point for this work was the suggestion from the teacher that a class of eleven and twelve-year-olds might grow some tomatoes for the school Summer Fair when they would be sold to parents and friends of the school. The task involved sowing and caring for the plants, and groups of children within the class had responsibility for their own plants. There was much class discussion about the conditions which were needed for the best germination and growth, which led to a variety of group investigations. These included measuring growth, controlling for different factors which might be important for plant growth, and setting up appropriate tests. Such factors included the effects of altering the food provided, the amount of water and the temperature of the plants. Each group of children focused on one particular issue which they would investigate and made hypotheses regarding possible outcomes.

One group was interested in the importance of light in the process of growth. They knew that the leaves were responsible for manufacturing the food from sunlight and came up with the question, 'Why are leaves green?' The teacher used a prism to demonstrate how the various colours are present in white light and the children wondered whether the leaves only used white light. They hypothesized that if they stopped green light getting to a plant it would not grow properly, but they did not know how to go about investigating the problem. The teacher offered them some coloured plastic sheets and left the children to the task.

Initially they covered the plants with green plastic but could only see green light coming through. They concluded that green plastic let green light through but stopped the other colours; therefore the other colours should stop green light. The next stage in their investigation was to try different coloured plastics and observe the effects.

To isolate the plants from other light they devised cardboard tubes which fitted over the plant pot and the coloured plastics fitted in the top of those. Soon other problems arose, for instance how to test only for the effect of colour by ensuring that the same amount of light reached the plants. A light meter was employed to measure the light coming down the cardboard tube. The number of sheets of coloured plastic was varied for each colour until approximately equal amounts of light reached each plant. During this stage, one of the children suggested that one plant be covered with clear plastic to let all of the colours through, thus providing a control situation in case more than one colour was needed to support plant growth.

At this point the children felt they were ready to move forward with their experiment and went back to the teacher. He posed a further question, 'Suppose one of your plants is weaker than the others anyway. Will it still be a fair test?' Eventually they decided that there would be three plants in each batch. The group made predictions as to what would happen. The predictions for the effects of the different colours of plastic on growth were:

GREEN	Best
RED/YELLOW/ORANGE	Fair
BLUE/PURPLE (Night colours)	Worst

Over the next few weeks, they were surprised to find that the results were:

GREEN	Poor
RED/YELLOW/ORANGE	Good
BLUE/PURPLE	Poor
CONTROL	Best

Their hypotheses were wrong in this situation. Much discussion occurred among the children and between the teacher and the children. He eventually posed the question, 'When you look at something green, what colour light must be coming into your eyes?' Some children realized that green coloured things reflect green light and absorb the other colours, but others were unconvinced and had not firmly internalized the ideas involved.

At this point we leave the children with their problem. It has to be remembered that other groups of children were following other investigations, that other activities were occurring during the time these investigations were taking place, and that, apart from this scientific work, there were drawing and painting, reference work, and a variety of ways in which all of the work in progress was recorded. During this time groups of children shared their interim findings with the whole class. As the work on the topic drew to a close, each group shared their final statements and findings.

Some further developments of the plant investigations occurred but the above episode is illustrative of several points. The starting point engaged the children's interest. It was clear throughout that there were times when the children were making decisions about the way forward and other times when the teacher was intervening in a way which would extend the children's thinking without providing instant solutions. At several points it was evident that the teacher had considered possibilities and had in hand the appropriate materials to support the work. By definition, an investigation into growth meant that the work was spread over a fairly lengthy period of time, with regular short returns to carry out measurements, and longer periods of sustained discussion, experimentation and recording. Perhaps most important of all, the investigations were seen to be part of a continuing process.

A Visit to Worsborough Mill

Worsborough Mill is a 200-year-old working water mill which is half an hour's coach journey from the school. The class teacher decided, in the light of the topics on which the class of ten and eleven-year-olds had previously worked during their time in the school, that a day at the mill would provide a good starting point for the next few weeks' study. She made the necessary arrangements for the visit and considered possibilities for activities on returning to school. The classroom had a display of articles and books relating to bread-making, milling, corn and the historical aspects of Worsborough Mill. Apart from the materials which would always be available, she made sure that certain technical construction apparatus was there to be used as she anticipated the machinery would be an important part of the stimulus.

The visit itself was spent in looking at the mill building, its machinery and its environs. During the day, working drawings were made, notes were written down, and questions were asked of the curator as well as of the teachers.

It would be impractical to examine every strand of the work that followed but a few examples will be sufficient to show the breadth and quality of the responses. As with most visits, the first thing a child wants to do is record experiences. The opportunity to experience the noises and movement of a working mill, to see the carved names of men and women who were millers there over many years, and to handle the masonry and woodwork of the building informs the images and ideas of children far more than talking at them. The amount of work done on each area varied from child to child but all of the children, at some time in the next six weeks, were involved in historical research, scientific investigations of cogs and gears, art, writing poetry and descriptive prose, and reading connected directly with the visit. The interpretation given to the work had a reality caused by a reference back to the experience.

After initial drafting and development the historical research was presented on very large pieces of paper, interspersed with appropriate drawings. The children worked in twos and threes and the specific topic varied with each group. They chose, for example, the lifestyle of the millers in times gone by, the history of Worsborough Mill, the development of mills in the British Isles, and the process of milling.

The study of cogs and gearing led to a profusion of technical models. This began with some groups trying to make working models of the mill itself, including the sack hoist. There followed a series of investigations, some relating to gear ratios and others to the transference of power from one plane to another. The children recorded these not only through models but also in charts, working diagrams and written work.

Individually children wrote poems about their experience at the mill and illustrated them using water colour paints. This included various drafting stages before arriving at the final format and presentation. The language had a clarity and immediacy which were clearly influenced by the actual experience.

Some children did sewings, clay models and drawings associated with the visit. The resulting images were very real but more than photographic. They captured the essence of the original stimulus and personalized it within the constraints of the material being used. One group became involved in printing some large lengths of fabric using a block which they had cut themselves from a potato. The motif was of a piece of machinery they had seen at the mill and which they had drawn while on site. As the printing developed, the arrangement of the motifs and the colours selected suggested the patterns and movements associated with the working mill.

To appreciate fully the extent and quality of the response it is necessary to see the work produced. The pieces clearly show the diligence and persistence of the children. They show far more than simply writing about a day out. The teacher closely connected the children's previous experience of the materials available, their ability to make choices and their academic needs. There were times when there was no choice and all the class did similar work, as with the scientific work and the poetry. There were other times when children had some choice, as with the particular emphasis of the historical work and the use of specific art materials. The children were helped by the teacher to sort out their new experiences and to set them alongside their previous experiences. They were helped to select and order, to examine carefully and to clarify their impressions and understanding.

The urban farm

It is important to recognize the value of the immediate school environment in promoting learning. Within the school itself there are often opportunities for valuable educational activities. As children come into a school, it is often taken for granted that they are aware of the roles of the people within the organization and the way in which the school operates. In contrast, it is often assumed that by telling them how the system works the children will understand. The children will be much more involved in the reality of their school if they visit the boiler house and see the caretaker at work, if they visit the school office and are shown how to operate the telephone system and the photocopier and hear from the administrative staff what they do and why, and if they visit the school kitchens to find out how the school meals are prepared.

On moving out of the building itself, the opportunities multiply a hundred fold. Among other things there are local transport facilities and shopping areas, garages and factories, building sites and community buildings. All of these provide opportunities for learning.

A school on the edge of an industrial conurbation was fortunate to border onto farm land and the farmhouse and buildings were only fifteen minutes' walk from the school. The proximity of the farm to the school meant that each had already had contacts with the other. The teacher discussed with the farmer the possibility of a visit by her class, which was readily agreed to.

In addition the farmer mentioned that one of his old barns had a variety of farming implements and equipment which the school could borrow. With the help of colleagues the teacher eventually managed to transport a horse-drawn plough, a potato sorter, and various tools and implements to the school. She was able to gather supplementary materials from a variety of other sources including her home, her colleagues and the local schools' museum service. Two of her colleagues helped in creating a large display of the materials one evening after school.

When her children came in the next morning the excitement was very high. There was much talking, handling and looking which was soon followed by close observation work and writing. Questions were asked about the purposes of the equipment and the farming processes in which they were used. The book collection the teacher had gathered provided a rich source of information. The nature of the display tended to focus on past farming practices.

After several weeks the next phase of the work was begun. The class visited the farmhouse and outbuildings. In talking with the farmer and his wife they were able to build on the social as well as the architectural history of the farm and find out more about the setting within which the implements at school had been used.

The ensuing work embraced story writing set in the context of the farm, as well as recording and researching further information. The teacher had, from the start of the work, been sharing literature set in the appropriate era.

Then the work moved forward in time, and a second visit focused on the work the farm was doing at the present time. It was possible to see the various animals and visit one of the fields when the combine harvesters were collecting the crop. There was an increase in the understanding of the reality of farming at the present time. Maps were used to locate the extent of the farmer's activities, and plans were created to show different land use. The focus moved towards the geographical aspects of the curriculum.

Parallel to this, the display in school changed to accommodate the focus on current farming practice. At the same time, relating to the harvest work, some of the children baked bread and experimented with different flours and recipes. At each stage and in each area of study, a variety of ways of recording were used including maps and graphs, drawings, art work, and various forms of writing.

A significant aspect of the work which should be recognized was the importance of social relationships and mutual understanding. The farmland adjacent to the school was also adjacent to the homes of the children. They often used to play near it or on it. From time to time, the nature of farming meant that sometimes there could be potentially dangerous situations for the children. Furthermore, any damage caused to the crops by the children playing would affect the farmer's income. What the work with the farm did was to add a new dimension to the long-standing relationship between the farm and the school. The social issues involved were seen by the children as being more meaningful. To the children involved, it was seen much more as 'their' farm. They identified with it and became more protective towards it. If situations arose during the long summer evenings which the children felt the farmer should know about, they would go and tell him. The farmer would ask the school to cooperate at certain times in the year when he was working on certain pieces of land. The particular group of children were able to share their awareness with other children in their peer group who had not been involved in the visit. Both school and farm benefitted in the consolidation of their relationships and continue to work mutually together with the community.

Reflections

The three situations outlined above draw on three distinct starting points. The first centres on activities pursued by the children as a result of a real problem. They wished to grow tomatoes for the school sale and to maximize their yield. The particular group whose work was described took on an even more specific task. To do this it used equipment and matrials within the school and focused on scientific investigations.

The second set of work, while prepared for and followed up in school, was a result of a day visit by coach to an historical site. Here, while major historical ideas were developed, it is clear that other curriculum areas including art, language and science were an integral part of the study.

The final description used two different major stimuli. One was the local environment within walking distance of the school, the farm, and the other was the related equipment collected and displayed by the teacher and her colleagues. The curriculum areas which were central to that work were clear, but there was also the social dimension of the relationship among the school, the children and the farmer.

Although there were other avenues which the children might have explored in each case, within the constraints of the system, the teachers made decisions regarding the appropriateness of the work for their children. The feedback from the work as it progressed led to further amendments and changes of direction. The evidence of the teacher's role in planning is very clear, as is the creation of an appropriate organization to support the learning experience. The provision of resources in terms of equipment, usable materials, reference books and related artefacts of relevance supported and extended the work. There was also day-to-day discussion with colleagues regarding children, ideas and equipment. All of these structures to support the learning process occurred within the positive and caring relationships established between the teacher and the children.

While these specific starting points may not be appropriate in every situation, the general ideas can be considered by any teacher. Specific problem-solving which has relevance to the children can often be identified by the children themselves. Teachers can provide learning resources within the classroom which will stimulate ideas. There will be interesting starting points for learning within walking distance or a short coach ride, no matter where a school is situated. These alone will not satisfy the needs of the children but combined with appropriate planning and provision by the teacher, real learning will begin to take place.

Reviewing Progress and Assessing Achievement

It is clear from this and the previous chapter and specifically from the examples of integrated work given in the last section, that an integral part of the learning process is the teacher assessing and reassessing the class, group and individual activity and progress as the work develops. Nevertheless it is necessary to examine the notion of assessment more fully in order to set it in its proper context.

Any assessment of the work of the children will have to be made against the previously agreed school aims and objectives. These may broadly embrace the intentions that children will be continually encouraged to meet new situations and to acquire skills which will enable them to deal with those new situations. The skills will include the ability to make informed choices, the ability to constructively question and criticize and the ability to relate to other people. In addition there will be the more specific skills and objectives identified in the various curriculum statements and guidelines which the school has.

It has to be remembered that these broad aims and specific objectives have not been created in isolation either by the headteacher or by the staff of the school. As we have seen in Chapter 1 no individual school has the freedom to operate in a vacuum. The influences on the activities in the school include national government policy and statements, the perceptions of the local education authority and, in the United Kingdom, the attitudes and wishes of the governing body as well as the individual and group expectations of the parents. In addition the school has to take into account the broader societal pressures and the pervading ambience of other professionals operating in the field of education. It is within those over-lapping, and sometimes contradictory, parameters that the teaching staff of the school bring their own perceptions to bear. Further, in applying their professional awareness and knowledge, they take into account the particular needs of the children attending the school.

From this set of shared intentions, the school determines appropriate activities and experiences and provides a suitable learning environment. As we have seen earlier in the chapter, the class teacher plays a key role in influencing the quality of that provision. It is against all of those intentions that any assessment is made.

Day-to-Day Assessment

Within the classroom assessment is continuous and cyclic and is very lengthy. Teachers observe the children's actions and reactions as they pursue the various activities and experiences provided in the classroom. They record achievements, areas of work covered and areas of particular need on a day-to-day basis. The nature and amount of recording will vary according to the patterns established within each school. While such records need to be informative regarding individual areas of experience covered and individual academic achievement, they also need to be of practical value in improving the education of the children. However, if a major part of the teacher's time is spent in record-keeping and form-filling, it cannot be spent on curriculum planning, classroom organization and actual teaching.

In the examples used earlier in the chapter, the teachers maintained records specific to their children and task, however they followed a similar pattern. Where children were working in groups, the record of the broad area of work covered was enhanced by notes on individual difficulties and possible areas of extension as in the case of the work on tomatoes. With the work on the mill, although all children completed a piece of historical research work, this varied in its nature from group to group. The teacher was aware of which group had studied which area, and in this case record-keeping included notes made on individual children's abilities to research from books or other information sources. In both cases evidence was noted of individual understanding of concepts and skills, whether in the area of science or history.

Sometimes work being undertaken was at a class level. In the case of the farm work, all of the children had drawn and written about one of the farm implements. Similarly all of the children had participated in a discussion on the dangers of playing near farm buildings and machinery. Where it was felt to be necessary, additional notes were made concerning individual children. In these cases the notes included particular abilities or areas for development in drawing and group discussions. This monitoring of the children's work is part of the process of continuous and continual assessment carried out by the teacher of the children's learning and experiences.

Part of continuous assessment is through discussion with and observation of the children. These were clearly exemplified by the teacher working with the children on growing tomatoes. He provided appropriate support materials at the right time because he was aware of the needs of the children. He regularly checked out their understanding by asking questions and teasing out what they were thinking. When invited, children themselves will often make critically informed comments on their own achievements and understanding. They are able to assess honestly their application to a particular task and the standard of presentation against their own abilities. If they are given the opportunity they will explain points of difficulty in understanding new ideas. The way in which they describe their experience of the world can be very illuminating and offer a counterbalance to the teacher's perspective.

The work produced provides additional evidence of achievement and understanding, whether of skills, concepts, or materials being handled. The reports and technical models of the mill referred to earlier supplemented the discussions that had taken place while the work proceeded and indicated the understanding of gears and transfer of force from one direction to another that had taken place. Similarly, the water colour pictures which were used to illustrate the poems showed the awareness and level of control of that medium that individual children had achieved.

The informed assessment of the child's performance and readiness for the next task is, as has been indicated, continuous. It will inform adjustments to the ongoing work. It acts as a clear indicator of the need to change or adapt the work programme as originally planned in the light of individual or group requirements. Thus, in the original programme, the teacher had various plans for extending the work on colour and tomatoes. Because of the response of the children in their experiments with the coloured plastic and the indications he had of their understanding of reflection and absorption of light, he took the pacing of the work from the children. To achieve what they did took longer than was anticipated but he accepted that it was better to have understood what they did than to encourage them to skim through a series of half-understood concepts and ideas just to complete a preconceived plan.

The importance of this day-to-day assessment cannot be overestimated. It is this which informs the longer term assessments discussed later in this section. Teachers' awareness and understanding of the children in their care are formed over time in the day-to-day interactions and observations, record-keeping and assessments in which they are engaged. These help in the task of attempting to match each activity to the needs of the child.

A Broader Perspective

There are significant points in time when a broader assessment is appropriate. One of these is when a topic is rounded off and is brought to a conclusion. At this point it is important that teachers review the achievements, or lack of them, for individual children in order that the next cycle of work builds on what has gone before. This may build on strengths or fill gaps in experience and understanding.

As well as individual needs, it is important to consider curriculum balance. If the previous area of work has focused on historical ideas, the next area may concentrate on science. If the work in mathematics which has just been completed dealt with two-dimensional shape, the next emphasis may be on number skills. Such balance will take account of work covered by the children when they were in previous classes as well their current class.

It is also essential for a school to consider how it will assess children's achievements in the various curriculum areas. While certain aspects such as mathematics and reading may appear to be easier to assess than others such as art and the humanities, it is important that an attempt be made across the curriculum. Even when assessment is attempted it may be that it is not directed at the concepts and skills relating to the curriculum area under consideration. In a survey conducted by Her Majesty's Inspectors, they observed:

> In about three-quarters of the schools the main form of assessment in science was the marking of the work that was recorded in the pupils' books. In most instances the marking was predominantly concerned with such items as spelling, grammar and neatness of drawing, rather than with an assessment of scientific understanding and competence. (DES, 1985b, p. 47)

More general comments were made regarding the need to match the assessment to the aims and objectives of curriculum areas. If the school objectives for the various areas of experience and understanding are clear and have been adequately formulated, they will provide a framework for such assessment.

Important sources of information regarding children's achievements are the permanent records held in the school. Reference to these, not only on receiving a class but also throughout the school year, provides the teacher the information which is relevant at class and individual levels. While such records can only provide a snapshot at a given time, they can provide another perspective against which a teacher's own assessment can be checked. In referring to records during the school year, it is also important to return to the colleague who made them. When the records were written, they will have been framed in the light of that teacher's experience of the particular child. They will reflect the teacher's frame of reference. Therefore it is important that a teacher reading the notes at a later date does not misinterpret them, but discusses them with the writer. In addition, these central records may be a summary of the more detailed records maintained by the teacher during the day-to-day work. Therefore it will often be possible to obtain additional information.

At regular times in the school calendar some focusing of assessment is appropriate. Such a review provides information for other teachers and for parents, as well as for the class teacher who is writing them. Included in those records may be some formal assessment or testing.

Formal Assessment

Many schools employ tests or school examinations as part of their assessment process. These may be standardized or devised and developed by the teacher. They may be norm-referenced or criteria-referenced. They are usually used at least once a year, but in some schools at a far more regular interval. The major focus for such assessment is on mathematics and language, with particular emphasis being given to reading. They provide a wide variety of information which can be used in different ways.

The results of standardized tests can help teachers to set their observations against a wider set of expectations and information. Some tests provide a diagnosis of specific skills and behaviour. They identify discrete areas of strength and weakness. Children with special academic requirements in particular curricular areas may be identified, included gifted and less able children. As a result a more appropriate allocation of resources and activities is made and individual remedial or extension programmes are devised and implemented. In the light of the additional evidence provided from tests, teachers review their intended programmes, reassessing their appropriateness and amending where necessary.

If testing is to be used, it is important that the teacher be fully conversant with the tests the children are to complete. Many tests have a specific purpose which should always be checked. There is no point in using a test unless it is appropriate for the purpose the teacher has in mind. The procedures for using tests are clear and precise. If comparisons of results are to be made with other children or groups of children, any deviation from procedure will invalidate the results.

It is easier to identify some skills, particularly in language and mathematics, and to measure ability and aptitude in them. It is very difficult to do the same in many other aspects of school activity, for example the performing and visual arts and interpersonal relationships. There are also many attributes which children are encouraged to develop but which are not easily subjected to formal assessment. It is not easy to test helpfulness, or growth in confidence, or increased perseverance. The apparent ease with which some skills can be assessed should not lead to over-emphasis on them. Ease of assessment is not necessarily indicative of relative importance.

Tests have a value but should be seen as one element in the total process of reviewing and assessing performance. If a school is to use specific tests, the reasons for their use have to be clear to the staff. It is important for the school to have developed a rationale which encompasses their application and that their use is consistent with the other work being done.

The information provided by tests will, to a large or small degree, enhance the knowledge the teacher has of the child. If an inordinate amount of time is spent on testing, it will leave little time for work. It may also result in the test rather than the needs of the children determining the curriculum. If the results confirm what is already known, this is of value to the teacher as support for planned action. If they contradict what is thought to be the situation, it will lead to a further examination of the evidence. Often tests will provide extra information which adds to the complex web of understanding within which teachers work when trying to provide for individual children.

In Conclusion

It is necessary that teachers do take stock and review what the children have achieved and where they might move to next but no one grows taller by being measured. If, as a result of the measuring, there is a change in diet, further growth may be encouraged. In the HMI survey referred to earlier, it was found that

> Assessment was usually undertaken to gauge children's level of achievement, but it was not often used as an indicator of the need to change or adapt work. (DES, 1985b, p. 46)

There is no one standard appropriate to all children of a given age. Ability and achievement vary with individuals and with different curriculum areas. Appropriate assessment should lead to a review of expectations and activities provided for individual children. While separate elements in the assessment process can be identified, it is a combination of those elements which have to be taken into account.

The school records, day-to-day teacher assessment and observation, children's work and standardized tests all provide evidence. An appropriate balance of these different elements in the assessment process will provide useful information. Whatever that balance may be, and it will vary from school to school, it is important that it relates to the aims and objectives of the school as a whole and to the aims and objectives of the particular curriculum area under review. As such it will be concerned with process as well as skills. If it does that, it will enhance the teacher's awareness of children's levels of understanding and thus better inform the nature of activities that are offered in the classroom.

In Summary

In building on the previous chapter, this chapter has focused on what actually happens in school. An examination of the curriculum particularly stressed the importance of acknowledging the variety of perspectives which are used to analyze what goes on in school. These various dimensions constantly interact and overlap to create a total picture. A broadly based curriculum framework, which embraces the whole range of activities that children meet, was examined. As well as looking at areas of experience, it addressed several important cross curricular skills and attitudes. Three case studies embracing a range of curriculum areas exemplified the nature of the classroom activity and the role of the teacher in enabling the work to progress and develop.

An essential part of the organic curriculum is that work in the classroom is part of a continuing interaction among the child, the teacher and the environment. In order to monitor what has been achieved, and therefore what should happen next, there is a need for regular review and assessment. In discussing this issue, the final part of the chapter completed the examination of the way in which the learning process is developed.

Chapter 7

The Rhythm of the School

The two previous chapters examined at some length the various factors which influence the learning process. A further important element in that process is the way in which time influences and is used by the school. In this chapter the intention is to examine the temporal dimension of the school and the way in which the patterns of time relate to those other aspects of the learning process already discussed to create a rhythm in the life of the school and the people in it.

The organic curriculum embraces several powerful ideas which inter-relate and interact to produce a complex and ever changing series of learning experiences. Significant learning requires appropriate and adequate time for working and for reflection. Even though some patterns of time are imposed upon the school, it is possible within these constraints to maximize the learning opportunities by arranging working patterns which complement rather than contradict the principal characteristics of the organic curriculum.

School calendars and timetables vary in specific dates, days, and times. Every school has unique patterns of organization. It is not these individual discrete models which are of interest. The intention is to examine some of the broad influences and trends which affect the nature and pattern of the work of the school.

The longest school time cycle with which children are involved is the total time spent in a particular school, from entry at the beginning of their school career or from a previous school to the time they transfer to the high school. Within that period of time are a series of other patterns. The school year, the term and, in the United Kingdom, the half term are the inter-mediate staging posts recognized in most schools. Shorter time rhythms are marked by the week-to-week and day-to-day routines. Even within a single day there are various patterns of breaks and working sessions. The various participants in the school have discretion over these time segments. The final decision may rest with the child, the teacher, the headteacher or authorities outside of the school. It is for the teacher and headteacher to make the best use of the time they control within any imposed constraints in order that the child maximizes the opportunities for learning.

The School Year

Within the state system of education, the school calendar and holiday periods are not negotiable. It is in the light of local education authority policies and national factors that the school has to operate. However, the particular grouping of children and the allocation of teachers are within the control of the school and come under the authority of the headteacher.

While various factors are taken into account such as the social and academic needs of the children and the expertise and wishes of the teacher, there is still an arbitrary element in the formation of a class at the beginning of the school year. A new class coming together with a new teacher has yet to establish its own set of norms and mores. These are conditioned to some extent by the expectations and patterns of learning and behaviour already established over several years by the school.

Certain groups of children may not be coming together for the first time. In a small school children may move as a cohort through their time in the school. Where children have already been in a class together, certain norms and expectations will have already been established.

In all cases the teacher's task is to bring the group together as a cohesive unit, a unit which will allow for the children within the class to develop at their own rates and in the ways most appropriate to them. One difficulty is determining the extent to which a specific individual's needs can be met within the group without compromising the needs of other individuals in the class.

Although that issue has been addressed in several ways in the preceding chapters, it is necessary to consider it with particular reference to the passage of time. The early interaction between the teacher and the class will tend to be more structured than the later interactions. As the year passes, the teacher will gradually increase the level of autonomy which the children have. This will vary with individuals. As children increasingly cope with organizing materials, choosing working partners and prioritizing tasks to be completed, so the opportunities will be increased.

The progression is not always linear. There is the need for consolidation of self-determined actions and activities, and further opportunities for increased autonomy are delayed until an appropriate time. On occasions, some children will not be ready to make their own decisions and there will be some regression and reduced opportunity for self-determination. Nevertheless, observation over time shows a clear development in the children's ability to take responsibility for their own learning.

The teacher still retains control by monitoring, challenging, suggesting and directing, depending on the circumstances. No child will have achieved total autonomy although some children require less directing than others. Looking at the class as a whole, by the time spring has arrived, the working relationship which now exists between the teacher and the children has a confidence and maturity which did not exist at the beginning of the school year. Many of the day-to-day organizational needs are automatically carried out by the children themselves. Materials are renewed and replaced, equipment is organized and checked and the routines relating to the use of space are well established. Many of the children know what they have to do before they even enter the classroom and return to ongoing work. Significantly, children are often aware of the need to obtain help and, when appropriate, approach the teacher for instructions or advice. The tentative start as a new group at the beginning of the school year is no longer visible. The confidence of the teacher and the children to work together and support each other is clear to see. The amount of time spent by the teacher addressing the class as a whole reduces over time, although it is still used when judged to be the most appropriate and efficacious style.

The Natural Rhythms of the Year

The rhythms of the year often influence the content of the work being pursued. Those rhythms may link to the natural pattern of the seasons. As the school year moves through autumn into winter, spring and, finally, into summer, so the work in the class will follow this cycle of growth. There is opportunity to investigate the natural world in its various phases. Overlaying those are the great cultural festivals and events of the calendar. In the United Kingdom, Harvest time and Christmas may provide a focus for work. The connections with the Christian church inform many of the practices relating to Christmas but the multicultural base from which the children come means that appropriate weight is given to the festivals of other religions and traditions throughout the year. The school is seen as part of a whole rich pattern of natural and cultural behaviour and diversity.

Within the school itself, recognition of the moving year is evident in the changing displays and learning centres. They change to reflect the festival or season or activity which is of significance at that particular time. Often this is within a particular class but sometimes the whole school works to a theme with each classroom and all of the shared spaces echoing the central idea under consideration.

The school year falls into separate terms; each of these have their own colour and pattern. The ends of terms are often marked by activities which relate to the school's wider role. There are open days when parents visit the school to see the work that is being done and, in particular, they have an opportunity to discuss their child's progress with the teacher. Social events include musical concerts or drama presentations performed by the pupils for parents and friends of the school. There are also social occasions for the pupils marking events in the school year which are of significance to them such as parties and end-of-school-year dances.

In the United Kingdom, where three terms are the norm, each term is punctuated by a mid-term break and the period on either side of that break is known as a half term. The variations in the calendar from year to year mean that any one half term may vary in length between four and eight weeks although the norm is nearer to six weeks. The half term periods often determine the time over which a class will pursue a particular topic. However, this is not always the case. The involvement of the children may mean that even after a break of ten days from school they will return to the work they were doing and soon become engaged in the activity again. At other times the response of the children may cause the teacher to change direction or bring a topic to a conclusion before a mid-term break. The importance of the teacher making the decision in the light of the particular circumstances cannot be overstressed. Nevertheless, teachers may establish initial plans according to the school calendar because the external constraint of the various holidays influences the rhythm and routine of the work.

The Day-to-Day Patterns

The length of the school day is normally determined by the appropriate external body responsible for the school. The pattern of working within that day, the timetable, is determined internally.

The way the headteacher and the staff perceive the aims of the school and the nature of the school curriculum strongly influences the day-to-day timetable and organization of the school. At one extreme is the very tightly structured timetable with many short working periods and specialist teachers for each of the subject areas. Children work at one activity for a given time and then move on to the next teacher and the next subject. At the other end of the spectrum is the school with no class timetable. The day is totally open with one teacher having full control over the pattern of working. The work is all at an individual level with each child changing activities at a different time. Most schools are in between those two situations.

A school structure provides a framework and a continuity within which individual teachers have some degree of autonomy and control. The structure allows a certain amount of flexibility for the teacher to extend and develop the working pattern of the children in the class. One such structure operates on a basis of four time segments for each day. The following section examines the possibilities and practicalities of this structure.

Purposeful interaction between the teacher and the child demands a variety of teaching and learning strategies. The nature of the interaction will vary from the teacher listening and drawing out ideas from the child, through questioning and suggesting, to prescribing and telling the child what to do. To accommodate this requires a variety of time segments and a facility for the teacher to be flexible in response to the particular situation.

When the day opens with a workshop of activities, with children working either individually or in a small groups on a variety of activities, the teacher tunes in to the work that children are doing. Activities include two and three dimensional art work, scientific investigations, and reference work relating to a variety of curriculum areas. The class teacher determines the range of work being pursued and the length of time that such a workshop will continue. There are several factors which will influence these decisions. One is the experience and confidence of the teacher to operate in such a way. Assuming that this is present, it is essential that the teacher takes cognizance of the children's ability to sustain such activities. Within a given session of, for example, one hour, some children within the class will need to change activity, perhaps writing for part of the time before continuing with a painting. Others will benefit from working on one activity for the whole hour, perhaps developing and writing up a scientific experiment. It may be appropriate for some children to continue into the next work session.

When children are motivated by the learning environment and the skilled interaction between them and the teacher, their commitment is very high. The process is not one of frantic action or of purposeless work to keep busy but of purposeful involvement. The level of expectation generated by the teacher is further encouraged by the group interaction and is allowed to flow unimpeded by false time barriers. As a result, children are using a high level of intellectual and physical energy. The quality of the process means that it is not possible to work continuously at that pace. There is a need for consolidation and reflection and for an opportunity to internalize the ideas which have been met.

At other times in the day the class will come together as a group. There may be time for quiet reading. Children may read to each other or tell the teacher about the books they are reading. At some point the whole class may be involved in a piece of writing; this may be concerned with specific styles of writing, for example, poetry or story or reference work.

Mathematics provides the focus for yet another time segment within which there can be several levels and types of activity to match the individual needs of the children. There are also opportunities to introduce new ideas to the class as a whole, to share stories and poetry and to work together on a variety of activities and interests. When appropriate the four blocks of time of the school day are subdivided to allow for shorter periods to be spent on a given activity.

Towards the end of every day, there is a time to ease down and for the class to get to know each other as people. A review of the day allows for the children to share their achievements and, just as importantly, indicate their intentions for the next morning. Before they leave school that afternoon, they and their teacher are clear as to what the first activity the next morning will be. So the rhythm of one day leads into the next day in a smooth transition.

The organization of the day, while apparently within a tight framework, remains very flexible. The key is with the teacher who has the autonomy to vary the pattern, structure and rhythm to match the perceived needs of the children.

The four time segments provide a basic pattern and establish a rhythm within which the class and teacher operate. In the United Kingdom, that basic pattern is punctuated by breaks in the school day. During the morning and the afternoon breaks there is opportunity for staff to meet and talk over coffee. During this time, some children continue to work at their tasks while most of the children go out onto the playground. Because most teachers of seven to twelve-year-olds have a high level of contact time with children, there are few occasions during the working day to converse with colleagues. These breaks offer times for relaxation, but significantly, the discussions and interchanges are centred on professional issues. These are brief opportunities to check out ideas, to share information and generally to engage in professional dialogue. The lunch break offers similar opportunities, but it is longer. During this time many teachers take part in extra-curricular activities by running clubs and societies which children may choose to attend. Similar opportunities occur at the end of the school day. The range of activities offered varies from school to school but may include chess, football, netball, guitar, recorders, choir and drama. These voluntary activities help to cement the relationships established between teachers and children in the school day. As the composition of such clubs is not identical with the class groups, teachers meet and take responsibility for children who are not in their immediate care.

Even within the working sessions there are variations in the basic pattern. There is a need for some scheduling of shared facilities such as the hall or gymnasium. The times when such facilities are available for a particular class will be given to the class teacher. The teacher then builds the rest of the class timetable around these fixed points. However, even here it may be possible for some negotiation between the teacher and the headteacher.

Some teachers may have expertise which other teachers do not have. Class teachers use colleagues with skills in specific curriculum areas for support. It also may be desirable for them to request some specialist teaching and therefore to establish an associated timetable. It is helpful to see this as an equation which has to be balanced. On one side there is the flexibility of time management for the class teacher and the children in the class. On the other side there is the specialist skill and knowledge which a particular teacher has and which can deepen and extend the children's awareness and understanding of that curriculum area. In this way it is possible to maximize the use of time to improve the opportunities for developing an organic curriculum.

The individual child in the classroom becomes part of that class, and the associated group expectations and norms influence activities. In turn the classes are part of the whole school. One mechanism for enhancing the school community is a regular meeting together and in the United Kingdom the school comes together in an assembly every day. The opportunity is taken to explore the wider setting of the school in the local community. Children and teachers share experiences they have had outside the school, and that sharing is valued by the whole school. There is regular opportunity to work together as a school through singing and listening to stories. Children regularly bring work into the assembly to show everyone. The assembly provides an opportunity for 'belonging', supporting and confirming the values and attitudes being developed in the classrooms. It also enhances the notion of continuity and oneness across the school.

It is clear that the notion of four time segments in each school day is only an underlying pattern. Organizational structures and school strategies such as timetabling of spaces and people, assembly and breaks overlay and blur the edges. There are also various external expectations and constraints on the allocation of time to various subject areas. Even within the times that are left to the discretion of the teacher, the differing needs of children mean that there will be a variation in the length and nature of working sessions.

The daily timetable is a structure or framework, not a straightjacket. It allows for the push and pull of day-to-day work and the need to respond to circumstances and opportunities. It helps teachers in both the planning and execution of their work. It recognizes the dynamic nature of the learning process. Taken in the context of the learning environment, of curriculum planning and balance, and of personal and physical resources, it supports and extends the learning opportunities which teachers offer to their children.

The Influence of the Child on Time

In examining the day-to-day structuring of time segments, it is obvious that the headteacher and teachers are the major influence on the form they will take, although the needs of the children are taken into consideration. The resulting frameworks are useful and powerful determinants of the learning opportunities offered by the school. However, one premise of the organic curriculum is that the nature of appropriate learning opportunities varies from individual to individual. Another premise is that the child should have a significant influence on the learning process. The school provides a framework within which groups operate. Within each group it is important that the individual is considered and, as has been shown, individual needs do influence the provision of learning opportunities. This applies equally in considering individual needs with regard to time.

If a class of children of the same age are given the same task to complete, it is very soon apparent that they will not all finish it at the same time. Some will finish very quickly. Others will quickly say they have finished but they have not actually completed the task which was set. Another group may take longer but complete the task within the arbitrary time allocated by the teacher. Yet a fourth group may ask if they can have more time.

If the same class were given a different task on another day some children would still fall into the same group in terms of the time required to complete the task. There would also be some individual changes. A child who finished very quickly on Task One may need more time on Task Two and so on. The response of the individual child to the task will vary for many reasons. It may be related to the child's ability or to motivation and interest. It may be related to the nature of the task.

One child working on a large clay figure is aware of the constraints and limitations of the material. She has a clear idea which she wishes to pursue. A record of the time she spends on task shows that on the first occasion she works for three quarters of a day with only two short breaks when she plays with her friends and has her lunch. The next morning she returns and spends a further half-day working on the project. Her involvement is clear, and, while away from the task, she has been reflecting on what she has done and what she will do next. The work is completed on the third day with another half-day spent fiinishing off and improving the model.

Another girl, in the same class and using clay again, is working on a much smaller model. Her representation of a scene from a story she is reading is completed in one session, one hour's work. A comparison between the two models will not show any differences in quality or technical skill.

Writing tasks also require different responses. A poem in its first draft takes perhaps one session. There is then the need for the child and the teacher to spend time together discussing the work. The boy writing it returns to it the next day and spends another hour reworking and improving his poem. Perhaps a few days later he again returns to the work and, after further discussion, prepares a final draft and produces a finished copy. The work has spread over several days, sometimes not being worked on at all.

A further example is in painting when children will begin their work and return to it for a session at a time over a period of two or three weeks, sometimes even longer. A final example is in mathematics. The time pattern to work on number practice skills is not the same as that required to work with mathematical investigations. One requires short, intense bursts, the other longer, more reflective activity and recording.

An examination of these and other patterns of working begins to show certain similarities. There is an initial need for exploration of the idea and the materials. This varies, among other things, according to the child's experience and knowledge.

At some point there is a direct and intense involvement with the teacher. In the case of the clay figure, the girl needed to call on the teacher's skill with the material. In writing the poem, the boy needed someone with whom he could discuss his work in order to clarify his ideas and language. In this way he was able to sharpen his image-making. The number practice called on the teacher's knowledge. The child did not have a skill, and the teacher had to share how the task could be completed.

Where the children became personally committed, where they were involved in the affective aspects of their development, there were long periods of intense work without the teacher. This is clear not only in the work on the clay model and painting but also in, for example, story writing and music-making when children have the skill to employ the power of the medium they are using to express their ideas.

It is obvious that these few examples do not all fit neatly into the time segments devised and implemented as part of the institutional organization. Within the frameworks operating at the class level, the teacher has to provide for individual requirements. Even if the majority of the class change activities, individual children can be allowed to continue their commitment to the work they are doing. Children are often aware of when they need to move onto a different task or when they can profitably continue with the same one. If commitment is to be maximized some decisions have to be made by the children and accepted by the teacher.

The large blocks of time identified in some of the examples may cause concern. Some people may feel that children are missing out on other activities. It is important to note that such situations will not arise every day. When they do arise, the most profitable course is for the teacher to allow the commitment and excitement of the child to be profitably channelled.

Balance in curriculum is not twenty minutes each day of a long list of curriculum subjects. It does not mean the allocation of a weekly timetable on a percentage basis to that same long list. It relates to the nature of the learning process outlined in previous chapters. If curriculum areas are of concern, then a longer time scale in assessing the activities and achievements of the child will soon put the individual time requirements into perspective.

The End of the Year

While the day-to-day, week-to-week and term-to-term rhythms of the school calendar all play their part in maintaining the dynamics of school life, the end of the school year has particular significance for staff, pupils and parents alike. The nature of its significance varies according to the differing perspectives of the participants.

Staff Continuity and Development

During the final term the teaching staff are involved in reviewing the year on an individual basis. Part of that review is an opportunity to talk at some length with the head of the school about their positions in and contributions to the life of the school. The nature of that discussion is explored in Chapter 9, and, while it is an important strand in staff development and therefore has significance for the school's development, it is only one part of the process. Along with that interview and with informal discussions among colleagues, all teachers will be personally considering their continuing roles in the school.

It may be that a teacher has worked for several years with a particular age group. While this has been successful, the teacher feels that a change to a different age group will provide professional development. In contrast, another teacher may feel that next year there is a need to consolidate some of the skills that have been acquired in the two years of working with nine and ten-year-olds and therefore prefers another year with them.

In extra-curricular work, where teachers volunteer to take various clubs and societies, some teachers may wish to relieve themselves of that commitment. Others may wish to increase the amount of work they are involved in. As the work is voluntary, it would appear a simple task to change roles. In practice this is not always the case. If teachers have been committed to running a football team, they are aware of the consequences of a withdrawal from that commitment for the children involved and, indeed, for the school. Any decision to decrease their involvement is not taken lightly. Similarly, a teacher may wish to begin a club or work in an area where other colleagues are already working. This requires sensitivity in moving into work with colleagues rather than appearing to take over. Several careful informal negotiations are necessary.

The approach of the end of a school year also gives an opportunity for staff to examine the contributions they make in particular curriculum areas. It is at this stage that it is most appropriate to review changes in teaching role and areas of responsibility. Teachers may wish to change the balance of specialist teaching they do. They may also wish to change the particular areas of curriculum responsibility they hold. In order to implement such changes, after initial private thought and informal discussion, some involvement with the head or senior staff members will be necessary. In some cases there may be a need for attendance at appropriate in-service courses. Even where teachers are not considering significant changes of direction in teaching or areas of responsibility, there is still a need to make medium-term plans for professional development.

It is clear that the ideas and practices which individual teachers are considering as the year draws to a close have implications across the school. Through informal discussion, formal review and school-wide discussions, the head and senior staff begin to have some indication of individual teachers' hopes and aspirations. Over several weeks of meeting and renegotiation, an attempt is made to match those expressed individual wishes to the needs of the school. It is not possible for every teacher to have every personal and professional desire met. Compromises are achieved. Eventually a plan of organization, evolves which takes into account the wishes of the individual teachers. This provides the starting point for the next cycle in the life of the school.

Continuity and Progression Within the School

The end of the school year has other implications for the teachers when the needs of the children for whom they are responsible are taken into account. Children's development is a continuous process, and schools have to build on the experiences and skills of every child. In particular, any points of discontinuity have to be minimized since they cause a break in the developmental process. Within all schools, the end of the school year means a change of routine and pattern for the children.

In most cases, where the teaching is class-based, a new year means a new class teacher. Although the norms of the school may be well established, all teachers have different personalities with particular emphases and attitudes to which children have to adjust. It should be said that the reverse is also true, and a teacher similarly has to adjust to a new set of children. Although change need not be negative because some children respond very positively to a new teacher or new organization, it is important that the school is consistent in its policies for minimizing disruption to the children's learning.

There is an established curriculum pattern which teachers have developed and negotiated over a period of time. Similarly, teachers have agreed on procedures in classroom organization and in the teaching of particular skills such as handwriting and arithmetic. The involvement of the staff at all stages means an acceptance of these broad policies. Significant differences in approach by different teachers are minimal. There is a thread of continuity running through the school which supports children and teachers.

The teachers are aware of the aims and objectives of the school and the particular targets for each year group, within which they take account of individual differences. As the school year moves into the final term, they check the general progress of the class and revise the targets for the rest of the year. The individual records which have been maintained over the year are drawn together. As discussed in the previous chapter, teachers implement some assessment procedures, the results of which are added to the records.

Eventually the current class teacher hands formal records of each child's progress, together with samples of work, to the next teacher. In order to lubricate the exchange of information, the transfer is not as formal as it sounds. There is ample opportunity for further discussion and reflection between the two teachers. In addition to a transfer of information at this individual level, there is also time given to discussion of curriculum areas covered at a class level. There is time to discuss the social groupings which have occurred and their significance in the work of individuals and the class as a whole. By this time, the receiving teacher has, in theory, a thorough knowledge of the individual children, their attainments and the work of the whole class who are to be received. However, this process of transfer is only one part of a continuous cycle. When the new school year starts and the teacher actually works with the children, there will be further consultation with the previous teacher in order to clarify what has occurred and to develop appropriate strategies for the future.

As well as compiling records for colleagues, the class teacher is aware that the end of the year is important for parents. Towards the end of the term there is an opportunity for parents to come to school and see the work their child has done. This is the final opportunity in a series which has covered the school year. The organizational arrangements vary with individual schools but allow a maximum amount of flexibility, offering opportunities to attend during the day and the evening. The intention is to achieve a high rate of attendance in order that the parents and teacher can exchange information about the child in private consultation. Sending a report of work achieved home prior to the consultation helps to promote mutually beneficial discussion.

The end of the summer term is marked by a variety of functions. There will be social occasions for parents and pupils such as dances, concerts and sports' days. End-of-year assemblies may include parents, but there will also be a special occasion when all of the staff, teaching and non-teaching, and the children meet together for a final assembly, marking the end of another year for the school community.

Transfer: Moving Into the School

For some children, the end of the year not only marks the move to another class but to another school. Some schools may take children from the start of their schooling, but for many children there is a transfer to a second school at seven or eight or nine.

For the children who transfer into a school which caters for pupils between the ages of seven and twelve, it is necessary to have some policy to ease that transfer. When such schools are on the same site, it makes it physically easier for the schools involved to cooperate. However, geographical proximity does not automatically mean sensitive transfer policies.

At the teacher level, some form of inter-school liaison within certain curriculum areas will be established. In practice, the major negotiation will be between the headteachers. Other members of staff, particularly teachers in the first year of the receiving school, regularly visit the feeder schools to become familiar with their organization and teaching approach. More detailed discussion occurs between the teachers concerned nearer the time of transfer and will refer to the individual teachers' records which are passed between the schools. This professional liaison is important and is paralleled by the activities which relate to the transfer to high school several years later.

Just as important, particularly for very young children, is the need for a policy for familiarization with the school they are to move to. As early as the December before they are to enter the school, children attend concerts, share assemblies and sit with older brothers and sisters and friends, and are taken by their current teachers to look at the school building, children's work and teachers' displays. The frequency of such visits increases in the final term. During that term, the teachers who will be responsible for the children on their transfer are identified. These teachers visit the feeder school and spend time with the specific classes and children they are to receive. Finally, the children come to the receiving school and spend one or two half-days working in their new school with their new teacher prior to the end of term.

In most schools there will be at least one occasion when the parents of those new children are invited to the receiving school. There they will not only meet the headteacher and senior colleagues, but also the teachers who are likely to be working directly with their children. An opportunity to look around the school will be accompanied by a slide show or video film of the work the school does. The structure of the occasion means that there are comfortable opportunities for informal discussion and the exchange of information, as well as dealing with more general questions and concerns. This is preparing the way.

On the first day of the new school year, the parents will bring their children to the school, confirm any routines the school follows, and check any final concerns with the new class teacher. By then the children have begun another part of their educational experience.

Transfer: Individual Families

There are occasions during the school year when families move area and children move schools. It is important that the transferring and receiving schools have an appropriate system for easing difficulties and maintaining continuity.

It is usual that when a family is due to move, one of the parents informs the school and, whenever possible, the name of the new school is given to the current school. This enables the transfer of appropriate records to the new school. If the receiving school is not known at that stage the records can be sent with the family. If this is not practical, when the child eventually registers at the new school, that school can contact the old one and any necessary transfer can then be made.

The main onus is on the receiving school. On the parents' first visit to the school, apart from meeting and talking with the head, they are invited to see the school at work. There is an opportunity for any questions to be asked by the parents. If possible the child spends a half-day at the new school before transfer.

On being transferred the child is placed into an appropriate group in the light of the information available. Apart from any records received, further information may be provided by the parents and by the child. Areas of particular strength or weakness are monitored carefully by the new teacher and appropriate individual tasks are provided.

In addition to any academic concerns the child is helped to settle in socially. If possible new friends from the same neighbourhood can be asked to look after the new child, sharing in the routines and patterns of school life. In the first few days the head or a senior teacher makes particular efforts to speak with and recognize the newcomer. In particular the class teacher will be looking for general opportunities to acknowledge the child's contribution to the class. Genuine early recognition and development of self-esteem are part of the process of induction.

Usually within a few days the new child has established some friendships and is beginning to contribute to the life of the class. There is an early contact with the parents to share the school's views and to obtain the parents' perceptions of the settling-in period. After that, although monitoring continues, it is usually of a similar nature to that which other children in the class receive.

Transfer: On to the High School

As one group of children are beginning their experience at a new school, so another group are moving out and on to the high school. All of the children will transfer to a high school at some point, and the age of transfer will vary according to the particular organization of schools in a given locality.

The high school will be a larger organization than any one of its feeder schools and may take from a large number of them. The logistics of transfer, liaison and continuity are a larger issue than at the previous stage of transfer. There are some issues which are of particular relevance to the high school and its role within the community. Other issues relating to transfer are of common concern to the feeder schools and the high school. The issue of discontinuity across phases and in particular between primary and secondary schools is increasingly well documented not only with reference to the social and pastoral issues. Recent research has indicated that:

> nearly 40 per cent of pupils scored less on the same test of basic skills in the June following transfer than they did in the final term in the old schools. (Galton and Willcocks, 1983)

The same research also showed that fewer than 30 per cent of the children made gains in all three tests of mathematics, language skills and reading in that same year. Recognizing the issue is not difficult but creating a solution is not easy when the realities of time, resources and energy are faced. Any strategy for transfer should not be seen in isolation but as part of a continual pattern of liaison, discussions and events. The point of transfer is a clear marker but is only part of a continuous interaction.

It is important that differences in teaching style, organization and, to some extent, objectives are recognized by both schools, each acknowledging the positive and negative aspects of its own way of operating. To reach even this stage requires patience and tact. It is particularly important for the feeder school to receive recognition of the work it has achieved. The children who transfer to the high school will have had six or more years of schooling upon which their future can be built. If this recognition is to be sincere, there is a need for the high school teachers in particular to be aware of what occurs in the feeder schools through visiting while the schools are in operation.

To enable such discussions to occur many schools have a variety of strategies. The heads of all of the feeder schools and the high school meet at least once each term. Sometimes other members of staff are present. The agenda is substantive but allows for informality and socialization.

In addition, regular subject-based liaison meetings allow subject teachers from the various schools to share expertise and develop common curriculum policies. This involves the sharing of schemes of work and development of agreed targets for children's work in all of the feeder schools. Some of the discussions are informed by the local education authority's policy. Other issues are specific to the schools involved in the discussion. The meetings focus on developing awareness and increasing knowledge of the differing roles each school plays in the children's education. The aim is to understand the complementary nature of the different phases and stages rather than seeing them as mutually exclusive and independent.

During the school year, the children will visit the high school at various times for a variety of reasons. Some schools share the high school facilities and take children to use the computer facilities that the high school may have. They meet some of the pupils already at the high school, look around the building and talk with some of the teachers. Parents have the opportunity to visit the school with their children on an open day, to see the resources and some of the work being achieved by the older pupils.

During the final term, the head of the high school and the head of the first year visit each of the feeder schools to meet children on their own ground to answer questions and to discuss a variety of matters with the feeder school staff. As the time for transfer nears, in some schools interviews are arranged. This is an opportunity for each child and parent to meet privately with either the head or a deputy head of the high school.

At the same time, the children's records of achievement will be completed and handed to the high school. The heads and staff of the various schools have determined the nature of these transfer records. The feeder schools want to provide all that is necessary. The high school is aware of what is useful. The records not only include an indication of work done and levels of attainment but also issues relating to the children's ability to organize themselves and the degree to which they are capable of determining their own learning.

If all of the factors relating to transfer between the two phases are satisfactorily achieved, then the problems of discontinuity will be minimized. Specific transfer structures help, but they need to be set in the broader context of interschool liaison. To develop such liaison is a long and important process. If the end of one period of schooling is to successfully lead to the beginning of another period, with progression rather than regression, then the necessary time and resources must be found.

In Summary

The rhythm of the school is influenced by various external factors, but within those constraints there are opportunities for the headteacher, other teachers and children to affect the structure and quality of the temporal elements of the learning process. The use of time, while only one strand in the total process, is significant in that it operates at every level, from the individual person, to the class, to the whole school. Indeed it is relevant to the wider context of the feeder schools and high schools.

At individual and class level a sensitive use of time can greatly enhance the level of commitment and standard of attainment which children achieve. Even within the constraints of organizing for a class of children, it is necessary, and possible, to acknowledge the different pace of work patterns which individual children exhibit. Complementary to those individual differences is the need for the class to develop a group identity and mutual dependence. Similarly at school level, a regular opportunity to meet together and share experiences or to work on a common theme will underline the interdependence of the various participants within the organization.

There are possible points of discontinuity which children experience during their school careers. At the end of each year children move class and some children move to or from a different school. Sometimes families move during the school year and children have to settle into a new situation. It is necessary for the staff of the school to give time and energy to the development of appropriate procedures and strategies to make such changes a positive rather than a negative experience for the children involved.

At times it may be difficult to disentangle these temporal elements from the total set of practices and attitudes prevailing in the school. Nevertheless it is important that they be considered since the rhythm of the school affects the mood and efficiency of staff and children alike.

Part III
Nurturing the Organic Curriculum

Chapter 8

Developing Organic Teaching

The discussion of the organic curriculum thus far has outlined its conceptual roots and its four elements, with close analysis of how the teacher and child ir.cract and description of how organic teaching and learning function from a broader perspective within the school and across time. This chapter discusses how educators can view the process of achieving competence and confidence in implementing the organic curriculum. By drawing on the observational skills used in the previous close analyses and broad descriptions of children learning and teachers teaching, educators may develop their abilities to implement such an approach. If the view of this curriculum in action described in detail in Chapters 3 to 7 is a desirable goal, then the following chapter will offer some ideas on how it might be accomplished.

The necessary competence and confidence to implement the organic curriculum are the result of a complex undertaking not easily described in so many words. However, at the risk of possible overgeneralization, the broad nature of that process can be suggested. In no way can this discussion be interpreted as 'the recommended way to operationalize the organic curriculum' because there are no clear-cut formulae for its accomplishment. At base, teaching is an art with professional development having a highly aesthetic quality. Moreover, the intellectual, reflective, proactive teacher remains at the centre of the endeavour as a decision-maker keenly conscious of the 'why' behind professional behaviour as well as 'what' it constitutes and 'how' it is done.

Adopting a developmental perspective in describing this process of professional growth assumes that teachers intent on implementing the organic curriculum move through sequential phases which are qualitatively different from each other and each of which is dependent on the previous phases for its fruition. However, patterns of growth are also individualistic with variations depending on one's previous professional experiences, one's personality and one's beliefs and values. Moreover, progress is not the same in the development of all teaching behaviours, with certain ones more fully developed than others; nor does moving forward in the teaching process occur evenly across all skills or at a predictable pace in all areas.

Within such a framework this chapter presents a three-phase model of professional growth in organic teaching along with specific examples of what can occur at each phase of its development. While the quality of the children's work develops across the three phases, the focus here is on the *teacher's* growth and development and not on the children's. This change in perspective from the emphasis of previous chapters is critical because the process of teaching is the key to the organization and structure of children's learning within the organic curriculum.

Several cautionary notes seem appropriate to make early in a presentation of the complex process of developing an organic teaching approach. For anyone striving to achieve change in teaching practice, it is best to begin in those areas where one is most confident, whether these are described in terms of strengths in particular curriculum areas, preferences in instructional strategies, familiarity with certain resources or personal interests which can enrich the educational experiences in the classroom. The areas which are most difficult or challenging in one's professional activities are best left until later when one has sufficiently developed the skills and confidence which can then be easily applied.

Secondly, adopting specific behaviours associated with organic teaching, such as integrating curriculum content areas or basing learning activities on children's experiences, should not occur as ends in themselves, but rather as part of a carefully planned and reasoned analysis of how the teacher can best facilitate children's learning. Any decision to develop a particular characteristic identified with the organic curriculum occurs because it makes sense within the broad context of what one is striving to achieve in working with children.

A third caution to apply to the discussion here is an acknowledgement that there are indeed different teaching styles and different behaviours associated with them. These are selected in keeping with the goals identified, one's own strengths in teaching approaches and the needs of the children. Teaching in the organic curriculum reflects this diversity of approach because it is based upon conscious decision-making arising from the teacher's reflection. It is not a rigid application of directives regarding what is the preferred approach in all situations; the term 'organic' itself implies this flexible response to the living, ever-changing, complex phenomena within the classroom.

A Developmental Model for Organic Teaching

Viewing the professional growth of teachers in the organic curriculum as a three-phase process begins to explain the complex development of competence and confidence. To some extent, this identification of phases is arbitrary, but it serves to underline that there are particular points where teaching abilities in implementing this view of primary education are clearly different from each other; different qualities emerge in one's teaching and in one's relationships with children as one moves along in acquiring the necessary skills. However, the process of growth also appears as a continuum with certain characteristics present in all phases but in various degrees. Movement from one phase to another is more a matter of a subtle transition than a clean break.

The phases in Figure 10 provide example starting points for teachers who wish to undertake professional development related to organic teaching. As implied earlier, because of previous professional experiences, other intellectual opportunities and personality characteristics one teacher who begins to think deliberately about organic teaching and learning may be at the second phase in the process, whereas another may be at the first phase. There is no inherent value attached to where one is in the process since the purpose behind the use of phases is to facilitate clear description of the steps. The model is not an exact one because professional development is not a neat, linear experience. Teachers may demonstrate behaviours associated with different phases and may move in one direction or the other depending on the goals they are trying to achieve, the children's earlier learning experiences and achievements and their own experiences and confidence in a particular area of the curriculum. It is also quite likely that growth in organic teaching is a recursive process with particular cycles repeating as one takes on more and more of the characteristics associated with such teaching.

Figure 10: *Phases in implementing the organic curriculum*

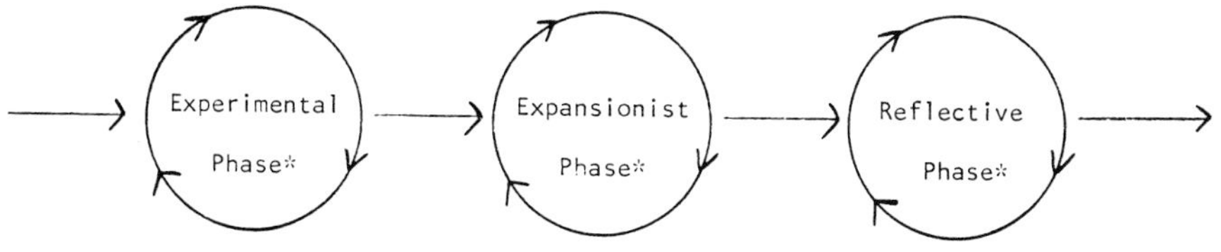

*During each phase, the teacher observes and analyzes what has happened and decides to continue development there or to move to the next phase.

The first phase is termed the 'experimental' phase. At this point teachers undertake individual lessons which reflect one or more of the various elements of the organic curriculum: child-centredness, an experiential base to learning, the integration of content areas or an emphasis on process skills. To be sure, in many cases all four elements will be naturally interrelated, though teachers will probably focus their planning, practice and reflection on one of them for the careful development of organic teaching. The lessons teachers design may occur for only a short period of time per week, may involve only certain curriculum areas where teachers feel most secure or where it is most likely children's learning would progress or may be discrete attempts to develop particular teaching skills.

Based on the results, teachers may revise the approach in future efforts, may broaden the application of what has been successful into more extensive work or into more areas of the curriculum or may reevaluate the degree of interest in pursuing further professional development in the direction of organic teaching. The 'experimental' phase reflects the need for teachers both to refine skills before using them more broadly and to try certain ways of teaching before making any extensive commitments.

Once teachers have had numerous successes in implementing characteristics of the organic curriculum within individual lessons, they apply their own observation skills in examining what has happened and analyze the process in order to decide either to reinforce their practice and build their own confidence by continuing to implement such lessons or to move to the next phase. If they choose the latter, they enter the 'expansionist' phase. With the solidifying of particular teaching practices there can now be wider application of organic teaching in more areas of a school's curriculum and consequently over longer periods of time.

There are several characteristics in teaching which appear at this point. The 'expansionist' phase may incorporate more of the elements of the organic curriculum at a given time. For instance, children may be observing what happens to jars of milk left for three days in different environments, recording and organizing their observations and describing in writing the sequence of events. They are working in many curriculum areas in the course of these activities, they are developing their process skills and they are clearly operating from first-hand experience. Teaching in this mode will likely encompass a greater part of the school day and the school week since school subjects and approaches to them are being reconceptualized.

During this second phase in implementing the organic curriculum teachers analyze and reflect more deeply upon what has happened in the curriculum process as a whole while the children have been engaged in particular activities. They examine the interrelationships among the characteristic curricular elements and appreciate how critical each element's support of the others can be. The implementation of organic teaching is now both more extensive, covering more periods of time, and more complex, involving a different way of looking at children's learning and at the professional decisions which facilitate it. Yet, it is because of the successful experiences teachers have had with individual lessons which perhaps stressed only one or two of the elements that this level of expertise can be reached; the results of those lessons have provided the building blocks, so to speak, upon which a more inclusive approach can now be based. The teachers' growth deriving from these earlier experiences has led to the ability to conceptualize the curriculum much more broadly.

As with the first phase, teachers observe and analyze what occurs during several of these longer and more complex curriculum sequences. After the experience of success, there is as before the need to decide whether to continue in this vein in order to solidify teaching practices or to move on to the more demanding requirements of the next stage. When sufficient competence and confidence are achieved so that success is virtually assured on every attempt, teachers will easily move into the next phase of implementing the organic curriculum.

The third or 'reflective' phase differs from the others because of the integration of organic teaching into the total classroom experience of the children. There the teachers' general style becomes 'organic' because in nearly all of the teaching situations such is the approach which is used. However, this is not to say that teachers rigidly follow a prescription or dictum; rather, the easy, automatic and natural decision-making process leads teachers to select the approach most appropriate for a given task or goal, with the result that 'organic' practices characterize most of the day.

A key factor lending distinction to this phase is the quality of teachers' thinking. This thinking arises from a coherent view of the purposes of education, the way children learn and the effects of particular practices on how children attain what we desire for them. Teachers in Phase Three begin and end each decision with thinking or reflection. Before action is taken, the situation at hand may be compared to previous situations which are similar; the results achieved then are considered as a plan develops for shaping the present and unique challenge.

While there is a deep intellectuality permeating teaching practice at this level, reflective teachers are also in charge of events. Instead of simply reacting to opportunities which may arise for incorporating organic teaching into the curriculum, as may characterize what occurs in the first phase, teachers now are proactive, deliberately setting up the environment so that a certain kind of learning can take place in particular directions. This structuring is careful, well thought through and without the undue restriction which often accompanies teaching not founded on organic principles. Because the repeated achievement of such a balance between valuing child-centredness and also acknowledging the importance of teachers' professional decision-making is such a delicate and demanding process, the intellectual qualities of teachers are called upon in significant ways. Moreover, the idiosyncratic nature of the task as it emerges in various contexts implicitly forces thought and reflection, rather than blind adherence to rulebooks or even guidelines.

Parallel to the influence reflective teachers have upon the learning of children is the direction they have over their own professional development. In this phase, teachers' intellectual skills control when, where and how professional growth will occur; inspiration or suggestion from others is not necessary, though such contributions are certainly enlightening. These teachers are independent and able to move forward in practice on their own, but without being oblivious to helpful direction from others. They have adopted a way of life which feeds on itself for continued growth and which is evident in how they approach both their work with children and their own learning.

How this pervasive thinking and reflecting translate into actual teaching is predictably difficult to describe. Several key phrases, however, communicate the general character of what is unfolding as such teachers interact with children. Firstly, they structure their work and organize their tasks within broad frameworks. In curricular terms, these may be called units, topics or themes. The teachers habitually demonstrate all four elements of the organic curriculum as they plan and implement activities, not as deliberately included components but as characteristics which naturally accompany what they deem appropriate for children. They view time broadly, for example assessing curriculum balance from a weekly or monthly perspective rather than from a daily perspective. They focus upon all kinds of learning, academic and social, and stress their interrelationships. And they assess children's accomplishments and their own from many points of view.

The discussion of this three-phase model of organic teaching suggests a natural evolution as the teacher fully develops confidence and competence at each level. Once the dynamic process begins it seems difficult not to proceed and to achieve the degree of art and craft necessary for the implementation of the organic curriculum.

The next sections of this chapter will describe particular teaching practices which may be associated with the three phases just outlined. These examples will give further direction to those educators who choose to organize for learning in ways this book has described. However, these are only examples, selected from many possibilities, which can suggest to professionals how they might proceed in following their own paths to the teaching practice they desire in their work with children.

The Model in Practice: Phase One, The Experimental Phase

Examples

As described earlier, the first phase typically involves individual lessons for a short period of time which stress perhaps only one or two elements of the organic curriculum. A very simple activity in this category could involve children writing down their observations of what occurs when they investigate the effect of a magnet. Having collected a variety of objects including perhaps paper clips and iron filings, they experiment to see which objects are magnetic and what effect the magnet has on them. First-hand experience is more evident here, as well as study in more than one content area of the curriculum since children are combining scientific work with practice in clear note-taking. Indeed, it can also be argued that a process orientation plays a part; the observational, organizational and writing skills developed here will transfer to other tasks children will face in school and later in life.

A more extensive example of Phase One in operation centres on a display of hyacinths. These are placed in the classroom on a Monday morning and the children must select two out of three activities designed for them by the teacher. They can either paint the flowers, write a descriptive paragraph based on what they observe with their senses or write a poem expressing how these flowers make them feel.

Several characteristics are present here which reflect an early experiment with organic teaching. The children are allowed to select which two of the activities they wish to complete, but the range of options is limited to the three the teacher has offered. The time commitment required for the children to complete their work may be no longer than two hours, though it is also possible an entire morning or afternoon session could be devoted to it. The activities can stand on their own, with little connection required to the rest of the curriculum for the children to gain benefit from the experience. At the same time, many avenues exist for further development of concepts in art, the clear recording of observations or creative expression if the teacher should choose to expand this lesson.

This example of three related activities recalls the discussion in Chapter 3 of the elements of the organic curriculum. It demonstrates how teachers may easily incorporate one or several elements without extensive planning, a large investment of time and resources or curriculum reshuffling.

The children have the opportunity of first-hand experience since they can see, smell and touch the hyacinths directly, both as an initial impetus to the set of activities and as a reference point while they work. Because the hyacinths are the obvious common theme of the three activities, there is integration of curriculum areas even though the children may be keenly aware that they are 'doing' art while they are painting and focusing on language while they are writing. The integration may broaden if the children use what they have learned in the first activity while they are involved in the second activity; making such connections would reinforce their understanding of how intellectual experiences can flow from one to another and how human efforts are often integrated because they relate to larger topics or problems.

A third element present here is a process orientation since the children are acquiring abilities which will be called upon both in future schoolwork and as they confront descriptive and expressive tasks in their daily lives. Further, to the extent that individual children may find intrinsic enjoyment and challenge in artistic endeavours or expressing their thoughts and feelings through various language forms, one could claim that these activities are child-centred. The options presented may also reflect the learning style needs of particular children. Thus, a simple set of teacher-identified tasks can represent all four elements of the organic curriculum to varying degrees.

The two examples described here show how a teacher can function in Phase One of the development of the organic teaching process. Much of the classroom environment and the teacher's approach remains the same. Yet, both of these examples begin with first-hand experience provided to the children, though this element does not always have to be the starting point.

The teacher may simply recognize the interest the children already have in frogs by asking them to share their excitement and to list descriptive words associated with frogs in order to develop their awareness of adjectives. The spirit of the organic curriculum would be supported in that the teacher was building on the children's interest and experience which they brought with them into school. Similarly, another starting point for the development of organic teaching skills may be the incidental integration of content areas when teachers refer to other material while they are focusing on one subject. An emphasis on a particular process skill can also serve as an appropriate place for teachers to begin development in Phase One; this may occur in just one short lesson, such as having children explain the decision-making process they used in designing a scientific investigation.

Analysis of these examples demonstrates how readily more than one element of the organic curriculum appears in teaching practice once a teacher carefully incorporates a first element into the activities structured for children. It is almost as if the introduction of one element naturally pulls with it the others because they are so intricately interwoven within the concept of the organic curriculum: when a teacher has children examine insects closely as a precursor to expressive work, the lesson draws upon first-hand experience and also recognizes at least two subject areas, language and science, while addressing an important process skill. From this perspective, then, the evolution of teaching skills seems to occur as a teacher naturally works and explores the potentialities inherent in the immediate task.

The two descriptions offered for Phase One also indicate how small-scale, practical learning experiences for children reflect the nature of the organic curriculum while they lay the groundwork for its future development. These activities are progressive in that they can be part of a longer-term development of the teaching process and can encourage such continued growth. Yet, on their own, they promote significant learning for children because they allow for sufficient work with ideas and are highly relevant to the school's goals.

Guidelines

Several guidelines may be helpful when working to develop the teaching skills associated with Phase One of the model for organic teaching. At the risk of oversimplifying what is still a complex set of professional decisions regarding the promotion of children's learning based upon sound psychological and sociological principles, a partial list of these guidelines follows.

The teacher should:

1 Identify a concept or skill which children need to develop and which can be achieved through any one of several instructional strategies.
2 Select a particular element or elements of the organic curriculum upon which to focus during instruction. The element chosen should fit in comfortably with the intent of the lesson rather than be added merely to provide a facade to a familiar task.
3 Incorporate the concept or skill identified in 1 above into a discrete lesson or set of learning activities from which children may choose one or several to complete.
4 Confirm that the lesson so designed authentically reflects the element or elements of the organic curriculum selected for emphasis in 2 above. For example, the teacher might ask whether the structured lesson actually does promote a process orientation to learning or whether it really is child-centred.
5 Limit the scope of the lesson so that demands upon time, requirements for material and human resources and dependence upon experiences in other parts of the curriculum are not extensive.

Adherence to the intent of these guidelines allows the teacher to experiment comfortably with organic teaching under controlled conditions. The limited duration and extent of the experiences promote frequent stopping points where observation and analysis occur; the resulting self-evaluation and redirection provide the necessary checks to ensure that there is appropriate implementation of organic teaching.

The Model in Practice: Phase Two, The Expansionist Phase

Phase Two is primarily an expansion of the individual lessons which might have occurred in Phase One into longer, more interrelated and more complex instructional sequences incorporating more elements of the organic curriculum simultaneously and across time. A teacher may examine and analyze curriculum objectives, activities and materials intended for children over several weeks or months. Components which relate to each other may then be reorganized so that children may more readily capitalize on the advantages to learning offered by the integration of content areas, the use of direct experiences, an emphasis on basic process skills and the acknowledgement of their interests and needs. Alternatively, the teacher may design an instructional unit for children which draws on the elements of the organic curriculum while addressing the goals set by school and government officials. This reorganization and expansion of already established learning activities occur most easily when flexibility in sequencing is available to teachers. Three examples may suggest how this process takes place: the use of learning centres, the organizing of learning around school trips and the designing of project work.

Learning Centres

Teachers may establish one or several learning centres within the classrooms. In the American setting, these centres demonstrate Phase Two of the organic curriculum because they represent a reorganization of objectives and activities into a format which recognizes what children need for effective learning to occur. Yet, the centres also respond to the pressures for accountability and the demands of meeting minimum competency levels because they incorporate what is deemed essential for all children to achieve and because they provide opportunities for the mastery of given skills, concepts and processes.

The learning centres may focus either upon skill or concept building within a particular content area of the school curriculum or upon a set of skills and concepts which relate to each other in reference to a topic or theme. Thus, a visitor could see a learning centre in one classroom which helps children to 'Think Metric' or 'Play with Words', while in others there may be centres related to 'Sailing our Waterways', 'Jack and the Beanstalk' or 'Peanuts'.

Each centre contains within it a series of activities or tasks which the children are to complete. These activities or tasks may be quite similar in format to what the children have previously faced in different content areas of the curriculum, but their inclusion in one centre, under one roof so to speak, lends a new character to them. Their interrelatedness is thereby stressed. Their presentation as a unique package for learning, including a range of materials and often operating separately from whole-class instruction, also encourages children to work independently and to acquire responsibility for their own accomplishments. As a result, the centre can facilitate both the cognitive and personal-social development of children.

The centre may serve as an introduction to study in a given area, as reinforcement for work already under way or previously studied or as an extension of the classroom curriculum which thereby enriches the children's learning. Indeed, the teacher may design the centre so that it is relatively free-standing in reference to ongoing classroom experiences or is interwoven with what is happening in the central classroom curriculum.

The children may be required to complete all activities presented in the centre in a particular sequence or only to select a certain number to complete. The children's performance in the centre will also be influenced by the level of competence which the activities demand; a minimum standard could be established for all or activities could be structured with an openness permitted in responding so that all children could complete them successfully but on their own levels, as in having them write paragraphs describing the growth of a bean plant which could represent different levels of language sophistication or vocabulary development.

The teacher who uses learning centres may carefully set up tasks which each represent a key component of study within a topic or theme and which are carefully arranged so that children can move smoothly from one to the next. In this sense, they parallel what programmed instruction offers to the classroom; children are required to move through all the activities in the given order, but they may do so at their own pace and with as much review as they desire.

If the tasks set for children are presented as a range of options from which the children may choose, the specific learning experiences will, of course, vary. However, the teacher has determined ahead of time that no matter what the children's choices are, they will attain the goals established for the centre. The structure in this case differs from the above because the teacher's goals differ. Choice as an organizing principle is more appropriate when the design of the centre focuses on reinforcement or enrichment of the central curricular experiences. On the other hand, if the centre is to serve as an introduction to work required of all the children, that is, if it is to 'teach' the children, a defined sequence of particular activities may be necessary, although some choices may appear within them in order to accommodate learning style differences among children or to capitalize on their individual interests.

A third approach to conceptualizing the tasks in a centre includes what could be called 'self-individualizing' activities. These usually focus on the development of process skills or draw heavily on children's first-hand experience. For instance, children may record their observations of insects living in a terrarium, categorize a collection of shells according to sets of criteria they define or write up the results of investigations they have conducted. The very nature of these activities produces an individualistic response; children participate in an individualistic way because they differ in their levels of process skill development and because the experiential base for the activities is perceptually grounded and thus personalized. Normally all children are able to participate to some level of success because the activities involve further development of those abilities already present to some degree in all; what they experience is expansion in learnings where by definition no maximum level can ever be reached.

In addition to promoting the teacher's abilities to function in the organic curriculum, the learning centre assists children in developing those skills necessary if they are to work comfortably in such an environment. The structure the teacher gives to the centre in terms of how children move in and out of doing work there fosters the growth of individual responsibility in obtaining necessary materials, beginning activities, checking work and recording progress. More structure, more detailed directions and frequent monitoring would occur in the first learning centres used in a classroom, but later the structure can relax with fewer detailed directions and less frequent monitoring required. Through practice children also learn how to determine when they need assistance, when they have completed work satisfactorily and the quality of what they have achieved. Attainment of these abilities is critical if children are to find success and pleasure in working in organic learning environments. Moreover, the degree to which they progress here can facilitate the teacher's confidence and subsequent growth. Moving toward the organic curriculum is an interactive process among all of those in a classroom.

Learning centres therefore exhibit many characteristics. As the teacher uses this instructional format, it may be well to keep these in mind as a guide for decision-making.

Typically, learning centres:

1 Meet children's needs at a given stage of development.
2 Meet children's interests at a given stage of development.

3 Reflect an accurate application of skills and concepts from the content area or areas included.

4 Build on children's previous experiences and encourage them to work from the first-hand experiences provided.

5 Accommodate a variety of learning styles.

6 Incorporate many ability levels.

7 Have clear directions, with step-by-step instructions.

8 Require minimal teacher introduction.

9 Require minimal teacher monitoring.

10 Encourage children to assess their own progress and to evaluate their own learning.

Learning centres represent Phase Two in the development of organic teaching because they offer the teacher many options for decision-making. In contrast to the examples in Phase One, organizing learning around such centres has significant curricular implications, from the design and management of the classroom environment through the integration of subject areas to the selection of materials and the use of time. Yet the structure of the learning centres allows the teacher to expand practice while maintaining substantial control over the options until competence and confidence build sufficiently to encourage movement into Phase Three of organic teaching.

Field Trips

A second example of the 'expansionist' phase of organic teaching is the organization of learning around school trips. This practice is cross-cultural with the 'field trip' and the 'school journey' long functioning as integral parts of primary education on both sides of the Atlantic. What differentiates the field trip as a manifestation of the organic curriculum from its use in other learning environments is the way in which it is incorporated into ongoing instruction.

The field trip can become the pivot around which the teacher organizes much of organic learning. As such, it has an integral relationship with the curriculum intentions set for children. It is a central focus for the provision of experiential learning because it gives children opportunities to see places and events and thus to observe first-hand natural and social settings and the daily occurrences of life within them. They can note how various sea birds nest in high cliffs, how farm animals care for their young, how the set-up of power plants exemplifies the division of labour among workers or how a flour mill functioned a hundred years ago. Beyond this rather passive function, the field trip may also provide children with occasions to perform tasks not available to them otherwise; on a camping trip, for example, they may pitch a tent for the first time or climb a mountain ridge. The process skills also inevitably operate since in the course of experiencing events the children use and perfect their abilities to observe, to communicate, to make decisions and so on.

The traditional content areas of the curriculum also find their way into the sequence of activities surrounding the field trip. Through the focus on real daily events in authentic environments information, concepts and generalizations from subjects areas are integrated and placed in their human contexts. The field trip thus encourages children in the acquisition and practice of content-area learnings as they might confront them in everyday life. And, because the children are observing natural and social events and are actively involved in meaningful tasks associated with them, they are likely more interested in the learnings to be developed. Thus, all four elements of the organic curriculum are present in the field trip.

The field trip becomes an effective vehicle for designing activities which incorporate the characteristics of the organic curriculum over a substantial period of instructional time. Teachers first select a site for the field trip with which they are very familiar. If they have learned of a field trip possibility from a colleague and consider that it has much potential for the learning of the children in their charge, they visit the site first themselves in order to confirm its relevance to the educational programme they are offering to their particular groups and in order to identify the range of activities which might be appropriate to present to the children.

Out of this substantial knowledge base, teachers relate the skills, concepts and generalization of the curriculum to the opportunities presented by the field trip in terms of providing children an experiential base for such abstractions, an opportunity for them to practice what they have already learned and a controlled situation in which to see the connections between school-based learning and complex yet everyday tasks. In essence, the teachers develop a strong rationale for this set of learning experiences and outline the purposes it will achieve and, perhaps even more precisely, particular content area objectives it will address.

Teachers then sequence the learning activities possible for children into three categories. They establish the activities in which children should participate before they actually visit the site of the field trip, those which are appropriate for the children at the site itself and those which will foster children's learning after they have returned to the classroom.

Certain activities may be prerequisites for children if they are to make the most of what the field site has to offer. For instance, a trip to a remote location where they might be hiking would require that the children have already developed map skills so that they may be able to determine their location at any given point, as well as the type of terrain they might face and the range of possible routes from which they may select. Or, children may need to identify ahead of time interview questions to ask of people they will meet. Another example demonstrates the importance of prerequisite knowledge if the field trip is to have maximum impact. If the focus is upon the variety of marine life in a particular area and the differences and similarities among species as they care for their young, obtain food and provide for shelter, it might be necessary to have children develop background about what they might see. Children would also need to have developed understanding of how different animals carry out their basic life functions in order to know what to look for and to comprehend that which they might see.

The activities in which children can participate during the field trip would be of two kinds, those which encourage them to become thoroughly involved in the experiences at hand and those which lay a foundation for work that will continue in the classroom after the children's return. The first type recognizes the traditional rationale for field trips in the school curriculum because they provide children with the active involvement necessary in order to learn most effectively. Such involvement encourages the children's academic motivation, recognizes their individual interests and helps them take full advantage of learning opportunities which may be difficult to arrange in other situations. The second type acknowledges that children acquire abstractions best when they already have the related first-hand experience upon which they can build. The teachers must be cognisant of and provide for the on-site activities essential if children are to move along smoothly during the later, more abstract, learning activities.

If children visit the seaside in order to observe closely the topography and to identify geological changes which are visible in the worn cliffs, then they must actually look at the land formations, point out the layers in the rock formations and walk along the farmland which may be adjacent to the cliffs leading to the sea below. Only in this way will they have the first-hand experiences which the field trip can uniquely give them and from which later abstract learning can draw. These basic experiences are the *raison d'être* for the field trip, even though the way in which individual children perceive a situation will vary and the particular details they observe may differ.

Teachers may also set the children to specific tasks while they are at the site in order to facilitate later work which will expand on these beginning experiences. The children may sketch what they see as an aid to their memories when they undertake more detailed exercises in recording their observations later in paint, fabric, clay or pen and ink. They may also jot notes to themselves which will be useful in their subsequent descriptive and creative writing. In response to their teachers' suggestions, they may listen to the sounds of a particular location, focus upon smells and textures, ask certain questions of guides or obtain appropriate samples and materials. At the time, these tasks may or may not directly facilitate the immediate experiential involvement of the children, but they are critical to the longer-term development of what the children have experienced into substantial and important learnings.

Upon their return to the classroom, the children will expand these initial experiences in many directions. Certain learnings will be easier for them to achieve because of the experiential base; the raw materials, so to speak, for abstract learning to occur, will be in place. For example, if children have visited a farm, their later conceptualization of 'mammal' would more clearly develop than if they had not been able to view first-hand many examples of mammals. Similarly, a visit to a power plant during which they would observe many departments in action would facilitate their understanding of how fundamental the division of labour is in the functioning of modern industry. They would call upon their own observations and those activities in which their teachers may have involved them in order to develop their comprehension of key concepts and generalizations of the primary curriculum.

In addition, specific on-site tasks can lead children to expanded work in the classroom. It is here that one might see the process skills of the curriculum actively developed. If children have been intensely involved and have found what happened to be meaningful, it is likely that they will want to react to and extend this exposure into expressive work or to pursue answers to important questions they have raised.

The sketches or notes the children bring back serve as starting points for expressive work in art, music or writing. However, these are not the only input to children's efforts; as the children attempt to render what they saw and experienced into some medium of expression, they will need to consult more than just their own memories or notes. They will need to refer to books which will explain further what they saw and thus make their task simpler, to compare their interpretations with what others offer in order to determine accuracy or to answer questions and to seek guidance from teachers in order to assure completeness in their work or to resolve problems which they might confront. As always, the teachers may need to nudge children into these processes if they do not naturally move into them as they carry on with their work.

A child who is painting a seagull in flight may find the depiction of the wings more difficult than simple observation would have originally suggested. Photographs and other paintings of birds, along with scientific and literary descriptions, may prove useful. Moreover, this problem could lead to study of the wing structure of birds and the role of the angle of wings in flight. On another level, challenges in using materials and tools may lead this child to a consideration of how to mix paint pigments, how to handle the fluid qualities of watercolour or how to readjust the plan for the painting in order to accommodate an error or mistake in judgment. In such situations, the child's growth in problem-solving skills can take on real meaning as far as the child is concerned. It may then be more likely for the child to appreciate what growth has occurred and how to apply these skills in other contexts.

The field trip, too, can lead to the development of children's questioning skills. The intense involvement during the on-site experiences often raises questions about how things work, what caused something to happen or why events occur as they do. If the children cannot immediately answer their questions, they may pursue them in the classroom later; thus, questions from the field trip may be the impetus for follow-up work. The children may research material in texts or learning resources, or they may set up their own investigations to perform in the school. Rather than providing grist for the intellectual mill, the field trip in this regard is a springboard for subsequent cognitive activity, a springboard, though, identified by the children and of great meaning to them. Pursuing this work hones children's ability to ask key questions and to answer them effectively, important process skills in any curriculum.

It is clear in this discussion that the specifics of what individual children experience on the field trip or in related activities may be diverse. Because experience is the central component of the field trip, individuality of perception is inevitable. Further, when growth in process skills is the instructional objective, variations in addressing those processes are not only probable but also desirable since each child is at a different point on the developmental continuum of a given skill and effective learning must begin where the child is. Yet, while there is such diversity, all the children will be able to achieve those objectives identified with concepts, generalizations and skill development because there is no one way to attain such learning and because, from a developmental perspective, the levels of understanding and the competence in skills may vary legitimately.

Learning in the context of the field trip takes on both cognitive and personal-social dimensions. Because the role of children's attitudes can be so significant in their learning, it is often difficult to separate the cognitive from the affective; the two become interwoven. Yet, in certain respects the field trip offers opportunities for children's growth in areas outside the traditional academic curriculum.

Because teachers may be with children for longer periods of time than in classroom settings, there will be occasions on a field trip for guiding appropriate behaviour in the larger community, for assisting in the resolution of interpersonal conflicts or for explaining societal expectations and introducing ways to meet them. Some children may need help in talking with adults other than family members or teachers. Others may have difficulty handling the gentle teasing of their peers. Still others may not realize how important manners and personal hygiene may be in human relationships. The field trip may be both the time when such issues arise and the opportunity for children to learn how to deal with them in an environment removed from the structured classroom and more related to everyday life.

Most examples of field trips include visits to sites some distance from the school. The field trip has traditionally involved the rental of buses and the expenditure of significant time away from the classroom. However, the characteristics of organic learning which the field trip offers are evident in outings which may occur very close to the school building itself. Walks in neighbourhoods surrounding a school, careful observations of plant and animal life on the school grounds or in a wood nearby or organized visits with the school secretary, caretaker and administration reflect an integrated curricular approach stressing the development of process skills which uses experience as a central focus drawing upon children's interests.

The many possibilities inherent in the field trip for fostering children's learning and their vast curricular implications indicate how the teacher is demonstrating Phase Two of the organic curriculum. The foregoing discussion may even suggest that the field trip depicts the organic curriculum fully functioning at Phase Three. However, if the field trip serves as the organizing structure for a carefully delimited segment of school time with only several preparatory activities, a few on-site tasks and follow-up work of specific duration, it exemplifies the organic curriculum at Phase Two. To the extent that teachers incorporate a wide selection of the possibilities inherent in the field trip as a slice of life and anticipate, develop and expand upon them, the field trip becomes the starting point for organic teaching and learning at Phase Three. The field trip conceptualized as child-motivating experience which facilitates specific later abstract learning and the development of individual process skills across several curriculum content areas is at Phase Two. The field trip which blends into the curriculum fabric as one of many ways to provide experience in a child-centred, integrated, process-oriented approach to teaching demonstrates Phase Three.

Expressed yet another way, the Phase Two approach places the field trip at the centre of teacher decision-making since it is chosen to match specific predetermined goals. In comparison, while the teacher still has clear goals, in Phase Three the teacher is more aware of potential points of learning and moves with the experiences and dynamics of the situation. Phase

Three recognizes the field trip as a means toward a complex set of educational ends and thus subsumes it under a broader view of how to organize
for learning. The 'organic' dimension is more obvious in the sense that
teachers nurture learning in many directions at once, incorporate experience
as necessary to facilitate children's learning and capitalize on learning
opportunities as they emerge thereby reorienting curriculum sequence from
time to time. The teachers also acknowledge the individuality of learning by
providing for differences in development and in learning styles and by
including children's contributions to the shape of their particular curriculum
experience.

Because the field trip can characterize the organic curriculum at both
Phase Two and Phase Three, it may also serve as a vehicle for the teacher
who wishes to move from Phase Two into Phase Three approaches. Indeed,
as teachers become more and more comfortable with using field trips in the
curriculum through observation, reflection upon and analysis of their
practice, they will find themselves appreciating how effective such visits are
as starting points for wide and varied work with children. Rather than
viewing objectives and activities in reference to the field trip, they will
perceive the potential learning emerging within each instructional
experience, select the directions to pursue and design the activities to accommodate them. They will discover that not all avenues for meaningful learning can be identified thoroughly days or weeks in advance and that shifting
and expanding will comfortably occur as the children's learning grows and
evolves.

Project Work

Project work constitutes a third example of Phase Two of the organic
curriculum in action. With a long tradition on both sides of the Atlantic,
project work can be connected to Dewey's problem-centred approach to
teaching, Kilpatrick's project method and the organization of the
curriculum into units. It embraces multiple purposes for children's learning
ranging from the development and practice of specific basic skills (Wray,
1985) through involvement in defined processes in research and inquiry to
the attainment of personal-social growth, all within the context of children
pursuing questions and concerns of interest to them around a central topic or
theme. Indeed, social learnings are often a principal reason for using projects
since children will most likely work and cooperate in groups during many
of the activities.

While many other terms may be used to identify what this section
describes, there seems to be no significant difference among them in terms of

examining how such approaches are representative of Phase Two of the organic curriculum. As a result, the terms 'project work', 'topic work' and 'themes' will be used interchangeably.

A key characteristic of project work is the teacher's role in designing the goals, the scope of content which the project will include and the sequence in which children will pursue the various activities deemed appropriate. Since it can encompass a significant amount of curricular time, the teacher must carefully coordinate any prestated goals or objectives expected of the children with intended project activities. During the initial planning stage, however, teacher and children may negotiate the more specific focuses, identify the directions and resources for particular activities, describe the outcomes desired and determine the responsibilities of group members. Project work then proceeds according to the original purposes designed by the teacher and along the lines of the plan of activities developed by the teacher and children.

Flow charts of connecting ideas and related activities (Schools Council, 1983; Waters, 1982) may be useful to teacher and children alike as they conceptualize the project itself and even carry out their plans and evaluate the results (Wray, 1985). Such charts may also permit a teacher to justify the project work as truly representing instruction in the various content areas, emphasizing the basic skills or incorporating the important thinking or process dimensions. In addition, they can help the teacher anticipate and hence provide for what is likely to occur and what should occur as a minimum as the project work unfolds.

The four elements of the organic curriculum operate clearly during project work. Because topics or themes typically serve as starting points in project development, the integration of subject areas occurs naturally. As children study the topics or themes representing rather broad concepts, they will need to move into content which draws on many parts of the traditional curriculum. Projects on city birds or Indians easily encompass contributions from many content areas.

Since the children do play a role in selecting some activities and refining others, the project recognizes their particular interests. The project can also accommodate individual children's strengths and weaknesses in the original design of activities and in the assigning of group responsibilities. Thus, to the extent that children are active learners and influence the specifics of the tasks they pursue, project work reflects child-centredness.

Project work also offers a process orientation. In carrying out what may be long-term exploration and inquiry, children develop and enhance their abilities to ask questions, solve problems, use resources, organize information and express ideas. One could argue that only in the course of such work could a teacher focus effectively on these processes since the time requirements for their development are usually substantial, since a meaningful context may be necessary for children to acquire such abilities and since the relationships among processes are essential if they are to be seen as useful and are to be applied appropriately to tasks later in life.

The definition of topics or themes for project work frequently draws upon children's interests in the world and everyday experiences. As a result, the element of first-hand experience will become central in the pursuit of project activities. For example, if birds are the focus, children may observe them from the classroom window or on the school grounds; stuffed birds would also provide the children with opportunities to look and to touch. An energy topic would most likely include an examination of the amount of electrical or gas consumption in their homes or in the school, along with a listing of those appliances which use each form of energy; if children raise questions regarding energy costs in different months of the year or from home to home, project work involves investigations, yet another type of first-hand experience.

Because project work organizes learning over much instructional time and because it often relates to everyday interests and tasks, it may also include field trips appropriate to the topic or theme which provide children with a clear experiential base for their learning. Therefore, how a teacher thinks through the organization of the field trip can also enhance the overall design of project work. The two versions of Phase Two in the development of organic teaching, field trips and project work, can thus be mutually supportive.

As the teacher undertakes project work in the context of the evolving organic curriculum, several guidelines operate:

1 A topic or theme is identified which relates to the nature and interests of the children and provides balance and continuity within the total school curriculum.
2 The varied purposes for project work must be recognized and clear objectives identified.
3 There needs to be a design or structure for project work which indicates the scope of content as well as the range of possible learning activities and how they interrelate.
4 The integration of the various subject areas of the curriculum must be authentic in reference to the general topic or theme.
5 The children should add their contributions both to the sequence of activities and to the way in which they carry out those activities.
6 The duration and direction of project work must key into its original scope while also flexibly acknowledging the motivation and developing interests of the children.

7 Project work must achieve a closure satisfactory to all participants, in consort with evaluation procedures which recognize growth and foster future development.

As with the field trip, project work may serve as a vehicle by which a teacher moves from Phase Two into Phase Three of the organic curriculum. In situations where the teacher carefully controls the shape and direction of a project according to present goals, planned avenues for learning and identified products, the approach reflects Phase Two. With increased involvement in project work, supported by observation, reflection and analysis, the teacher develops competence and confidence in such practice. As the teacher flexibly designs the focus for children's work, incorporates their evolving interests, needs and abilities and follows multidimensional paths for learning not all of which can be anticipated, Phase Three of the organic curriculum begins to appear.

At this stage, objectives still guide decision-making, but the analytic and reflective teacher recognizes that the possibilities for achieving them broaden as children work through the topic or theme. Such a fluid structure gives purpose and direction to the teacher's interaction with children while allowing for the potential inherent in the learning environment. The teacher at Phase Three has internalized the organizational frameworks used earlier in planning, carrying through and evaluating project work and readily calls upon them as necessary when designing and facilitating organic learning; but these frameworks now are aids to decision-making rather than specific guidelines for behaviour. The teacher at this point has a broad curricular perspective developed through rigorous analysis of and reflection upon teaching practice which serves as the basis upon which professional decisions are made to promote children's learning.

The Model in Practice: Phase Three, The Reflective Phase

Because a major intent of this book is to describe the organic curriculum in action at Phase Three, this chapter will not offer additional examples. A few comments, however, are pertinent here following the descriptions of Phase One and Phase Two.

Central at this stage are thinking, reflective, professional teachers. If guidelines or suggestions play a role in instructional decision-making, it is because teachers have internalized the spirit and intent of those guidelines in the process of devising personalized approaches to teaching. If all four elements of the organic curriculum are evident in the teaching and learning of children, it is because these elements automatically appear when teachers implement their decisions and not because a checklist demands that teachers include them. Where particular activities or organizational procedures may have guided teachers' behaviour in Phases One and Two, Phase Three places the buirden of decision-making squarely on these professionals. There are no sets of procedures guaranteeing success, but rather a way of thinking which teachers use in finding their own ways through the challenges and potentials accompanying their work with children.

Of course, the ease and confidence with which teachers may function in Phase Three are due in no small measure to the fact that these teachers have moved through the other phases and have learned those lessons well. They know well that the developmental nature of organic teaching requires a solid foundation of teaching skills and approaches and much experience in observing, analyzing and reflecting on their practice. With this foundation in place, teachers are ready to embark on the decision-making which demands that they address the needs of children, the requirements of society and the nature of learning in a balanced, organized fashion.

Teachers in Phase Three influence the very shape of the curriculum through their attention to the total picture of what could and should appear. Their perspective is both broad and deep. They must thus consider many curricular issues which did not seem as critical in the earlier phases. Balance among subject areas is important to monitor, as is balance between the requirements set for children by social and political authorities and those arising from educators' concerns and the needs and interests of children. Because the organic curriculum unabashedly embraces both academic and personal-social goals for children, teachers in Phase Three must grapple with how best to handle both so that they complement each other and so that they are congruent with community wishes. Teachers also have to face the issues raised by accountability; they must actively acknowledge the minimum competencies and skills which may already have been identified as they design the structure of children's learning and orchestrate the many factors which may influence that learning. The task is large and the challenge is great, but the rewards for having such decision-making so close to the children are that they may learn better and may consider that learning more meaningful. Teachers cannot help but approach such responsibility with care, knowledge, humility and enthusiasm.

Chapter 9

Professional Development and Awareness

Within the school there are many groups who come within the sphere of influence of the headteacher or principal. These include cleaning staff, school meals staff, clerical and administrative staff as well as the teaching staff. While they all play an important part in the development of the school, this chapter focuses on the teaching staff, as it is they who have by far the greatest influence on the development of the organic curriculum and indeed are directly charged with implementing it in the school.

The notion of staff development could be taken to imply some weaknesses or lack of expertise in the staff. To start from such a deficit model would not reflect the nature of what staff development is about. All the teachers are highly qualified professional people. They have undergone three or four years of initial teacher training and most of them have at least a first degree. They all have strengths to offer. They also have individual needs which require support. However the school itself has certain needs and requirements. Goals have to be attained, curriculum areas need reviewing and administrative and organizational tasks have to be efficiently completed to support those educational goals.

A central issue in staff development is that of balancing the needs of the individual with the needs of the school. To maximize learning, these must be in harmony because an emphasis on one or the other will benefit parts of the school at the expense of the whole. While staff development relates to an individual teacher's personal and professional development, it also relates to the development of the staff as a group and through this the development of the school.

However a key role is that of the headteacher. In the development of the school the head has made a major contribution to the establishment of existing parameters with regard to pedagogy and curriculum content over a period of time. It should be noted that part of the role has been defined both explicitly and implicitly to include the development of a 'school approach', a common ideology, an educational philosophy. Working on staff develop ment is an important element in developing an internal consistency within the teaching staff of the school and thus fulfilling part of the head's defined role. Within the United Kingdom's education system the role of the school leader is expected to embrace the notion of teaching along with adminis- tration. Although timetabled to teach for only a part of the week, the head is still perceived by the staff to be a teacher. Indeed this is part of the head's own role image. As such many of the suggestions and contributions the head makes are given value and legitimized by the staff. Yet staff development is not solely the prerogative of the head. Individual teachers will make their own contribution to this general development in the areas where they have particular strengths. With this in mind, we can examine the various strands which such staff development contains.

Group Development

In most schools dealing with children between the ages of seven and twelve, the organization of the teachers and children means that one teacher spends between 95 and 100 per cent of the teaching time working with a single class of children. The opportunity to converse with colleagues about educational issues, practices and problems and events is limited to coffee breaks and lunch breaks. In a school with an open plan design, such teacher-to-teacher interaction during sessions is more common and enables specific problems to be raised or even solved as they arise. The content of such interaction is often concerned with organization of materials, or the appropriate use of space and may involve the discussion of children's work and attitudes. It is usually brief and immediate and while such interaction helps to generate and maintain mutual support it only enhances the work of the school in a limited way. In a more traditional building such interaction is even more difficult to maintain.

Discussion

It is important that formal opportunities for developing shared ideas and shared goals are built into the system. The purpose of such opportunities will vary, sometimes taking an administrative role as a forum for infor- mation, at other times making decisions on certain aspects of the school's work. Similarly, certain classroom styles and strategies can be shared and the strengths of individual teachers can be used to support colleagues in the school. The regularity of staff meetings or discussions is important. They should become a part of the ongoing process of school development. Their frequency depends on particular needs and circumstances.

In one new school these were originally held weekly, at lunchtimes, and lasted approximately an hour. As the school developed and staff became more established such meetings were a little less frequent, about two out of every three weeks. From time to time a longer meeting after school was thought to be more appropriate and, with the agreement of the staff, this was arranged.

Other schools develop their own pattern. It is important that teachers' time is recognized as being of value. If too many meetings are held which are perceived by the staff to have little relevance, they may distance themselves from the proceedings. To avoid this not only is there a need for a clear programme and purpose but staff need to be involved in setting up the programme. While the head suggests and decides many of the topics to be examined, the staff are regularly asked to put forward ideas for discussion or development. Teachers with responsibility for a particular curriculum area across the school are both expected and expect to chair a session or series of meetings and suggest possible activities. Any aim or purpose in having a meeting should be made explicit so that the staff can judge whether anything has been achieved. The following sections illustrate some of the variety of format and content which is possible.

Often staff meetings are led by the headteacher. It is an opportunity for the head to put forward views regarding the way in which the school should develop. However every endeavour must be made to bring the staff into the discussion. An obvious format for such meetings is for a brief opening statement to be made, and then the topic is open to discussion and comment. The structure of the discussion needs to be given some consideration if the number of teachers who are to make a contribution is to be maximized. Sometimes a full group discussion is appropriate, at other times discussion in smaller groups with feedback to the main group can be more profitable. Sometimes the aim is to reach a decision, for example on a mathematics scheme or alternative organizational structure. At another time it is to share ideas and to go away and reflect on the points made, teachers absorbing them in different ways into their own teaching. Yet at other times the purpose is to practice and develop specific skills or strategies such as teaching handwriting or using specific mathematical structural apparatus.

A particular example of a topic for discussion in one school was the expectations staff should have of children with regard to the way they address adults and each other. It broadened quite quickly to include the way children conduct themselves about the school, and the influence of the home compared with the school on general behaviour, attitudes, manners and dialect which children exhibit. The outcome was not a dramatic change in policy or in any one teacher's attitude to the issues discussed. What the discussion did was to allow for a restatement of the head's position and the policy which the school has tried to follow over several years. It also allowed for the different approaches which staff had within that policy to be re-examined, restated and compared one with another. The most significant outcome was that it caused some teachers to reflect on and slightly modify their practices. It also reinforced the idea of individual professionals working within agreed goals and practices.

Not all discussions follow that pattern. On another occasion the teacher responsible for language development throughout the school prepared a series of meetings which were designed to review the reading policy which existed and to examine one or two specific suggestions which might be incorporated into the practices of all of the staff. A few days prior to each meeting the head and language coordinator met and discussed the proposed presentation of materials and ideas. Various papers were prepared and on some occasions staff were asked to try particular teaching strategies prior to the next meeting and to report back. In addition information on certain aspects of reading was given out for the staff to take away and use. The first two meetings asked why children should read and how we might encourage children to read. The third meeting focused on recent research into the arguments for and against listening to children read. After this there was a session which specifically looked at assessing the appropriateness of the book a child is reading and strategies for developing a good attitude toward reading. The next session was based on feedback from the whole of the staff and their suggestions provided the points which were to be discussed further. The final session concentrated on book-related activities and class management necessary to incorporate such activities into the general work of the school.

Obviously there were many aspects of reading not examined, but the six sessions did focus teachers' thinking and allow for significant personal and professional development. The common experiences and shared information suggested ideas and practices for staff to discuss informally over the next few weeks and months. They also provided a focus for discussion between the person with responsibility for language across the school and other teachers, positively enhancing their view of her role in the school. Most importantly it provided an opportunity for the language coordinator to develop her skills in managing and presenting such material to her colleagues, allowing her to take responsibility at a different level from that of a class teacher. While each session stood alone, the series was a strong contribution to staff awareness and practices.

Children's Work

A different approach to discussion is the use of children's work as a focus for thinking. Teachers brought samples of work relating to a particular curriculum area to a staff meeting, for example, two pieces of art work, and commented on why they thought they were 'good' and what they thought the child gained from doing the work. This concentrated the staff thinking on to two central elements which underpin the school's philosophy. Firstly, there was the acknowledgement that teachers do make judgments about children's work and, as that is so, they should be aware of the criteria they use in such situations. Secondly, that while a finished artefact may be pleasing to look at, it made the teachers more aware of the thinking that went into the making of the finished artefact and the benefits that accured to the child in the process.

On another occasion when examples of children's poetry were used they centred on the way in which children at the younger end of the school produce work of a different sort from that of the older children. The teacher leading the session was also able to raise questions of appropriate starting points for such work, ways of teaching poetry and the nature of poetry.

Other possibilities include sharing different styles of writing, science investigations, and mathematics. In each case practical ideas are pooled and used by individual teachers at some future time in their classroom teaching. More importantly, central issues about what the school asks children to do and how it goes about it are raised. Assumptions are challenged and reasons explored as to the value and importance of each of the activities being used.

In asking teachers to share work with colleagues in this way it is important to recognize that some individuals may feel vulnerable. The purpose of such sharing is to build on what is positive. Although teachers select which particular items to share, they may still be concerned about the reaction of their colleagues. Any negative reactions can set people back a long way. It is important to assess whether the time is right for a particular school to work in this way as it requires sensitivity and awareness from everyone involved.

Walkabout

Within the busy teaching day it is not always possible to stand back from one's own class and look at what is going on in the school as a whole. In 'closed' classrooms it is very difficult to know what is going on in other rooms, even if they are only next door. Even in more open buildings, assumptions are made that all teachers are aware of the practices of colleagues. This is not necessarily the case.

One way of seeing more of the school is to hold a staff meeting in a different classroom on each occasion. Another useful group staff activity is to walk around the school looking at the various classrooms. Each class teacher may spend a short time telling colleagues how the work on view in the classroom had come about, what was thought to have worked well and not worked quite as well, and how the teacher saw the work being developed further. Sometimes such a walkabout will be focused on particular aspects of the school's work, a particular curriculum area, the use of displays or the use of books. This sharing of experience helps in easing informal discussion over the next few months by making staff more sensitive to the particular problems, priorities and practices of their colleagues.

The comments made concerning sensitivity and vulnerability when sharing work are multiplied tenfold when teachers share their classrooms with each other. There is a need to choose the time carefully. It is not an easy option and needs developing through a variety of shared activities. If it is approached in a way which causes teachers to feel threatened the opportunity for development will be minimal.

An extension of sharing classrooms out-of-session is for colleagues to see each other working during school time. If the impetus for such developments comes from the teachers, the results will be very positive with a growing awareness of the strengths each teachers can share with colleagues.

Visiting Other Schools

It is important to extend horizons by visiting other schools. A normal arrangement is for teachers to focus on a particular aspect of school activity, for example, the approach to environmental work, mathematics or art. Then arrangements are made for pairs of teachers to visit schools with a reputation for good practice in the chosen area. For organizational reasons these may extend over a week or two. Each teacher may be expected to return to school having fulfilled two simple tasks. Firstly the teacher notes at least three specific items which are of value in his or her own teaching. These remain confidential to the teacher and are for personal use unless the teacher should choose to share them with particular colleagues. Secondly the teacher may be expected to identify three or four points which are pertinent to the specific issue being examined and which may be useful for the whole school to consider. These points may support or contradict present policy and practice.

The results of such visits are extensive. On returning to school, each pair of teachers, in talking about their experiences, engages other staff in informal discussions. The staff meetings following a series of visits have a new impetus as the teachers explore the relevance of the visits to current school practice. Although there is a specific focus for the visits, there are many wider, incidental benefits when teachers compare and contrast the nature of the school they have visited to that of their own. Finally, there is a boost to morale through the general opportunity to visit another school in school time.

Workshops

A further aspect of staff activities is participation in practical workshops. These either relate to a specific aspect of a curriculum area or focus on particular materials, their organization and application. The role of the general class teacher means, almost by definition, that any one teacher will have areas of experience which are less developed than others. While individual support from colleagues with specific responsibilities for curriculum areas is valuable in providing materials and ideas, it is also possible to call on each other to provide practical sessions which allow teachers to have first-hand experience of the handling of specific materials and ideas. If the necessary expertise is not present within the staff then colleagues from other schools or local authority advisers may make an appropriate contribution. Such sessions may include clay work, the use of threads and fabrics, mathematical activities, conducting science investigations, participating in improvized drama, practicing handwriting, and indeed may extend to any other aspect of school activity.

The level at which individual teachers meet such activities is related to their previous personal involvement with specific materials. One teacher may be an expert potter, another may have never touched clay. A third may be adept at movement or drama while a fourth may have never been involved with the performance arts. Each person has a different level of experience and competence for a given discipline. Nevertheless the sharing of a particular activity as a group makes such sessions very useful in staff development.

The direct value in participating in these workshops can be seen at several levels, with regard to the professional and the pragmatic aspects of the teacher providing such practical activities in the classroom. The teacher becomes aware of certain organizational possibilities or sees how the work in the classroom with, for example, clay can be developed further than on previous occasions. New starting points for work may emerge, or solutions to teaching specific skills and techniques may be clarified. The actual handling of materials and the physical involvement reinforce the learning far more strongly than just talking.

Even more important is the enhanced sensitivity of the staff to the influence of the use of materials on children's personal development. This is particularly clear in the arts where the aesthetic and affective aspects of children's growth are so important. By working with their bodies, painting, modelling, and using other materials teachers become more aware of the value of such work to the development of the individual. This experience not only enhances the personal skill of the teachers but allows them to experience some of the emotional and intellectual challenges, the problems and possibilities which arise when children are asked to tackle such work. They come to appreciate the continuous interaction between the person handling the materials and the materials themselves, each reacting to, and developing from, the other.

The benefits of such sessions are not only evident through the discussion generated at the time. The shared experiences create a point of reference for future formal and informal debate and discourse.

Major Initiatives

So far the discussion of group activities has centred on the development of individual teachers alongside particular strands of school activity which are already in progress but require some re-examination. Sometimes there is a need to make major curriculum or organizational initiatives. The way in which such initiatives are introduced, developed and reinforced is in itself interesting, but with reference to staff development it is sufficient to make three points.

Primarily, an innovation offers teachers with areas of responsibility an opportunity to extend their range of influence and to develop their skills of communicating with colleagues. They also see their actions directly changing practice in the school. In this context the head has to be seen as being in total support of the curriculum coordinators. Secondly, as the items are major departures from existing practice and not simply developments of old practice, it encourages a fresher level of discussion since nearly all of the staff feel that they are at a similar point in their development. Thirdly, and most obviously, since the ideas and practices are new, all of the staff increase their awareness of the content and pedagogy relating to the areas under discussion.

Innovation is relatively easy to implement but the maintenance and development of an innovation require continuing effort over a period of time. If such major initiatives are to take root, it is necessary for the teacher with responsibility for a particular curriculum area and the head or appropriate senior colleague to liaise very closely at every stage in identifying the area for development, in setting the scene and preparing the way, in implementing the innovation, and in developing this implementation over the next few years. It is not only in the interest of the school and the headteacher, but also of the curriculum coordinator, that the initiative should be successful.

From the Group to the Individual

Staff meetings and group activities act as a focus for re-examining practices in the school as a whole. However, as schools develop over several years and as children develop at different rates, so do teachers. Some staff take on ideas quickly, experiment, take initiatives and involve themselves in broader issues by attending courses, or attempt to influence certain aspects of the school's work. Other teachers are more deliberate or less inclined to change practices which they have adhered to for several, or even many, years. All teachers have their own particular areas of expertise and interest. Members of staff bring different professional perspectives, different personal backgrounds and specific sets of hopes and aspirations for themselves and their children. Therefore it is important that opportunities for discussion and development are made available at an individual level as well as at a group level. In the smaller school, a key person in this development will be the headteacher. However in many instances it may be a colleague who fulfils this role of support and encouragement.

The headteacher's role is, of necessity, partly administrative, but it is mainly one of a headteacher, a colleague with some experience and expertise who not only offers support but is invited by the staff to support them in their work in the classroom. While the head may often take the lead it is important that initiatives come from teachers regarding possible areas of interest and development. The teacher's perspective is as valid as the head's. Sometimes the head or other colleague is a listener, someone on whom the teacher can test and try out ideas. At other times the head works alongside a particular teacher, sees the issues at first hand, and provides a different perspective. This means offering support and encouragement as well as suggesting alternative approaches. While this immediate support is of some help to the teacher, the shared experience provides material for further discussion and analysis of content and style.

Specific Children

Discussion with individual teachers may focus on particular children in their classes. This may lead to the development of specific programmes of work or a detailed analysis of individual behaviour patterns. As each child presents a unique set of experiences and attitudes, relationships and behaviour patterns, it would not be practical to describe every situation but an example may demonstrate some underlying ideas.

On one occasion, the recurrence of behaviour problems with a twelve-year-old boy led to a three-way case conference involving teacher, head-teacher and educational psychologist. This was quickly followed by a further meeting which included the child's parents and the child. The outcome was a simple but specific behavioural programme, and, as it turned out, there was a marked improvement in the boy's behaviour over the next two months which was maintained until the boy left the school some eight months later.

The significance for staff development was on several levels. Firstly, and obviously, the teacher was involved from the beginning in discussion with the head and outside agencies. Secondly, the teacher was faced with a challenge in attempting a new idea which was to apply to that particular child in her classroom. The feedback was positive and this enhanced the teacher's standing with the child and class, but it also influenced the teacher's view of the educational psychologist. Finally, the head's role had been one of mediator, trying to move the teacher towards the idea of outside advice, the child towards an improved self-image and the psychologist to an aware-ness of the delicacy of the classroom situation compared with the clinical situation.

Curriculum Issues

Sometimes the cooperation between head and individual teacher is centred on curriculum matters. Help in providing materials, analyzing classroom organization, and reviewing curriculum content will take place on many occasions, during and after teaching sessions. Sometimes the issues will be small-scale and dealt with in a few minutes. At other times larger issues demand a more complex programme of support.

An example of specific curriculum work between the head and a teacher occurred in the field of movement. A teacher who was fairly new to a school and who had an interest in movement work was concerned about the content and style of her teaching as it was not an area in which she felt confident or had had much experience. It seemed important that practical support was provided alongside any theoretical discussion. It was agreed that each week the head would come into the class and for several sessions take the children for movement. This was to avoid the teacher being immediately put in a sensitive and potentially vulnerable position. During the sessions and afterwards, the head and teacher discussed the content, the various approaches and the balance of activities. The head explained why he was trying certain ideas, where there had been a digression and why he had chosen certain alternatives rather than others. Alongside this the teacher was provided with various articles and readings which not only offered practical ideas but also gave a theoretical basis for the nature of the work being undertaken. Gradually the emphasis was changed. The teacher began to take more of the lessons and the discussions centred more on raising her critical awareness of her own work. This was the first step. It is important that the head return to that teacher and re-inforce the ideas which have been planted and encourage their further germination and growth. The planting of an idea is not difficult; the continuing nurturing and development are if the plant is to blossom.

It is not only the head who can operate in this role as it is often other teachers who have strengths to offer. The head's task is to create a climate where colleagues who feel they can benefit from mutual activity know they will receive a sympathetic response to their proposals. On occasions teachers may be freed from their teaching commitment to work alongside colleagues in specific curriculum areas such as drama, art, and mathematics. Here they use their expertise to help extend the work of colleagues. This relates particularly to curriculum coordinators who can negotiate with colleagues to identify fruitful areas for such work. This mutual activity is much more likely to succeed when suggested by the teachers involved than when imposed.

It is important to recognize that any benefits are two-way with the more experienced teacher or headteacher learning as much and growing as much as the class teacher who originally wanted the support. The growth is through the sharing and solution of issues of mutual interest, not the provision of simplistic answers.

Forecasts, Plans and Records

Within different schools the expectation varies with regard to forecasts, plans and record-keeping which have to be submitted to senior colleagues. Whatever that expectation is, it should provide a further opportunity for the professional development of the teachers involved.

While some schools do not ask teachers to submit a written forecast or plan of the following term's work, any proposed visits or major centres of interest are discussed with the head. Here is another opportunity for suggesting possibilities and sharing ideas. For example, if a teacher is planning a visit to a Norman castle, she may feel confident in most areas of the curriculum. The head will discuss the general areas to be explored and may suggest support materials or new avenues for exploration. The teacher may not be sure of how to develop the scientific aspects of the work. At this point reference may be made to the colleague with responsibility for science. Similarly, teachers who are confident and competent in scientific aspects of a topic or study may call upon the person with responsibility for other areas of the curriculum where they would appreciate some advice.

In many schools teachers are asked to provide a written summary of the work they have been doing with their children. Sometimes this is a weekly or fortnightly record. In other schools it is required each half term. The timing is something which each school has to decide but there are certain principles which need to be recognized if such records are to have value for the teacher who writes them. Primarily, it is essential that the teacher has clear indications that it is of value to the reader. The head must respond to any requests for advice or points of concern made by the teacher in the record. Perhaps even more significantly, the head must acknowledge the quality of work outlined in the record and make positive responses to the teacher's endeavours.

Whilst some of the records of individual work which must be maintained are not directly relevant to this discussion of staff development, others are. An integral part of the summary of work discussed above will make reference to particular children as well to as specific teaching points or curriculum content. The reflection and appraisal by the teacher of what is being achieved away from the immediacy of the day-to-day teaching pressures are in themselves important for professional development. They may also be picked up by the head and provide starting points for discussion.

Individual Review

While there will be several times during the year when individual teachers and the head discuss matters in private, there is also the need for more formal meetings between the head and the teacher when a review of the teacher's role in the school can take place. While they have a recognized format, such meetings remain informal in nature, being a discussion of mutual value. The agenda is not generated because of a particular problem or difficulty with the teacher's work.

It is important that together the head and teacher review the work of the class for which the teacher has responsibility. This will cover curriculum content, teaching style, children's behaviour as well as the teacher's general feelings about how the work has developed. Closely related to this are the teacher's feelings about the next school year. For instance, which age of children the teacher would prefer to teach is of particular importance to the head and the teacher.

At this point the discussion often moves on to curriculum areas which the teacher would like to develop. Possibilities for in-service courses will be considered. Of course the question of attending courses occurs throughout the school year as do other issues, but this specific opportunity to review the situation means that longer-term planning can occur.

Since most of the staff make some extra-curricular contribution, for example to music groups, sports teams, book or chess clubs, this is reviewed. As such contributions are voluntary, the teachers can determine which, if any, they wish to maintain. Teachers sometimes welcome the opportunity to change the nature of the activity or, indeed, to be no longer responsible for it.

The head and teacher will also review the school-wide curriculum area(s) for which the teacher is responsible. They look at any developments which have taken place over the past year including specific initiatives made by the teacher in the relevant areas. In addition the individual teacher specifies particular targets for the forthcoming year. These may be very short practical tasks or long-term school-wide developments. While they are checked with the head, and some negotiations may be necessary, they will substantially be the targets set by the coordinator. The review becomes an opportunity to decide how that teacher's energies may extend and enhance those areas of responsibility in the next year including the practi-calities and possibilities of specialist teaching. Finally, there is an opportunity to review the teacher's hopes and aspirations and the ways in which the school can support any future career plans.

This thorough review of the teacher's contribution to the life of the school demands much ground work and adequate time, a series of meetings often being necessary to cover the areas outlined. The result is of benefit to the teachers in providing acknowledgement of the important contribution they make as well as their importance as people working within the school. It is also of benefit to the school in that medium-term planning is informed by a mutually agreed prospectus.

Informal Influences

Although the preceding comments have focused upon the more formal aspects of staff development there are many informal influences implicit in what has been said, in particular the general relationships which need to be established among the various members of the teaching staff. At all levels within the school, it is important to be sensitive to and aware of colleagues as people with their own perceptions, feelings and priorities. It is important to show an interest in their priorities even if these may not present themselves as being particularly relevant to the educational aspects of the schools development.

As has already been mentioned, the staffroom itself, during morning and afternoon breaks, before and after school, and at lunchtime allows for useful discussion and debate. The opportunity to converse with colleagues in this way not only provides mutual support but offers refreshment and relaxation.

In the staffroom there is a selection of reference material, recent publications, reports and teacher's manuals which are readily available. They are added to regularly and provide a source of information and ideas as part of the informal influences on staff development.

There are several times during the year when a school function means staff working during the early evening, for example at parents' interviews and musical concerts. These are usually followed by the staff meeting together socially and on such occasions the discussion usually turns to some aspect of school activity or development.

Similarly residential visits with children mean that in the late evening opportunities for social interaction arise. Here again staff development occurs within an informal setting. There are several times when colleagues explore, informally and at length, issues related to the school situation. These and similar opportunities lubricate the educational and professional interaction which is necessary among colleagues.

Induction of New Staff

So far the way in which the staff, and therefore the school, develop has been concerned with an ongoing situation, with people already established within the school. It is important to look at the way in which new members of staff are introduced to the school.

Immediately following appointment the new teacher spends some time in discussion with the head. In particular the head reiterates many general points which have already occurred both before and during interviews with regard to the general ethos of the school, and they discuss any anxieties and concerns which are currently on the teacher's mind. More specifically information is given regarding procedures, routines, ordering of stock, as well as information about the particular children whom the teacher will be teaching. They also spend some time discussing teacher expectations and sources of help and support. The teacher receives a full set of curriculum guidelines which are specific to the school. Prior to taking up the appointment at least two further visits will be made to the school by the new teacher. On these occasions the teacher makes further progress in becoming familiar with the building, discussing yet again the points raised earlier, and raising any new queries. At this stage a rapport between the new teacher and established colleagues begins to develop.

The teacher takes on a certain work load immediately on appointment, but if the post includes some curriculum responsibility the timetable for gradually taking over that task will have already been negotiated between the head and the teacher. In the initial few months the main task is to settle in as a class teacher and establish teaching credibility with colleagues and children. At the same time the teacher is assessing the current situation regarding any specific area of school-wide curriculum responsibility he or she may have. It is only after that assessment that thoughts can turn to changes or new initiatives.

A specific member of staff works with the new teacher to offer advice on school policy and practice. During the first few months the head and deputy head acknowledge the worthwhile contributions already being made to the school by the newcomer. Careful monitoring will attempt to ensure that any problems or difficulties, in whatever area, are recognized and dealt with at an early stage.

If a teacher is entering a first teaching post there will be a need for other, more detailed, support strategies and a different rate of taking responsibility. Before too long, if the usual pattern is followed, the new teacher is no longer that, but an established member of staff with unique strengths and weaknesses making a contribution to the life of the school.

Staff Development and the Process of Change

Staff development is the major, most significant, aspect of the headteacher's role since it is only through the staff that children's development and growth can occur. For a school to be alive to the continuous change within which it exists, the teachers must remain aware and informed. There is a need for long and short-term goals, for broad aims and initiatives as well as day-to-day management. The main focus of this chapter has been on the long-range perspective. Yet the short-term expedient action, the day-to-day activity, must be informed by the principles upon which the whole school operates. These principles are exemplified through the acknowledgement of staff development, indeed school development, as being about relationships and the recognition of each individual as having something of value to offer.

The general model of management which operates within the school should be one that is organic, changing with the needs of individuals and the needs of the school. Schools are about people and if people are to be helped to grow they need the appropriate setting in which to feel they can make a contribution to the changes that occur.

The main task of the head, and indeed of other members of staff, in helping staff development is one of talking and listening. In this way everyone will become more aware of the individual perspectives and priorities held within the school. In turn, and in time, will come decisions and policies which should contribute to a more efficient learning situation. In schools words are the main materials which we use. They are transient, constantly changing, constantly being refined. They lubricate the relationships among all of the participants in the learning process. They are used to stimulate ideas, to press awkward questions, to consider fundamental moral, political and educational issues. They should be used to create a setting within which the staff develop themselves.

Within what is a human and personal setting there are still structured positions, postholder or curriculum coordinator, and deputy head as well as the headteacher. These positions confer prestige and status on the holders, particularly if the head is seen to support them in their work with colleagues. They have clear job specifications and each member of staff is aware of the responsibilities of colleagues. If the school is in good organizational health it not only will run smoothly and achieve the tasks it sets itself, but will be strong enough to continually and critically review its performance.

Part of the development arising from that self-evaluation will be the satisfaction of some of the needs of the professional teacher which have been referred to earlier. These include support, praise and encouragement for each other, involvement in the overall planning of school strategies and policies, clear responsibility with the authority to implement new ideas, and the continuous development of professional awareness through extending individual experience and sharing expertise.

The aims of staff development are identical with the aims of child development. They are not based on making good a deficiency. On the contrary, staff should be excited by the professional setting within which they operate, developing a confidence in their relationships with each other, with outside agencies and with the children. They should, and do, take responsibility for organizing their own professional learning and development. It is the role of the headteacher to act as a catalyst for this to take place through recognition of good practice, encouragement of better practice and expectation of best practice from children and staff alike.

Chapter 10

Reflections

The organic curriculum is a living development which depends on the appropriate relationships and connections among all participants in the learning process. In particular, it is concerned with the interaction between the teacher and the child within the supporting school organization. It focuses directly on a child-centred, process-oriented approach to teaching which emphasizes the role of concrete experiences in learning and the integration of content areas.

The Roots of the Organic Curriculum

In the first section of the book we were concerned to set the appropriate context and parameters for a more detailed examination of the organization of learning for children. The historical background developed the assertion that elements of the organic curriculum have been evident in educational practice for many years and that the thesis we put forward arises out of a long and substantial tradition within education. The historical perspective also took account of the philosophical milieu which affects educational decision-making and practice.

The examination of issues related to learning and teaching supported the curricular approach presented in the remainder of the text. In particular, because this approach relates to many perspectives on how to foster learning, it was argued that the organic curriculum may provide an effective means of integrating these different theories via a practical application of their tenets.

The Nature of the Organic Curriculum

The second section was a substantive examination of the organic curriculum in theory and practice. The integration of the traditional content areas is a key characteristic of this curriculum. We explained the way in which this might be accomplished in some detail. Within this argument there is a central assumption that the exercise of specific human processes — for example, observing, questioning, decision-making, experimenting — enables children to learn actively and with attention to individual styles of learning. The discussion focused on how such processes are developed through concrete experiences and through learning related to the needs and interests of children who are thus placed at the centre of the educational enterprise.

From this general and theoretical analysis of the components of the organic curriculum and their interrelationships, we moved to a close view of how the organic curriculum operates in the classroom. In particular there was a careful analysis of classroom events in order to identify the under-lying structure of teacher and learner behaviours. Out of a few detailed descriptions of classroom life was built an understanding of the structure of the curriculum in operation. When combined with the concepts developed in Part I, this understanding formed the foundation upon which the teacher could develop the learning experiences of children.

A vital element in such an approach is the role of the teacher as curriculum developer. Even within the parameters set for the school as a whole, the teacher still has significant freedom to plan for the needs of children. The nature of that freedom and the way in which it may be trans-lated into practice provided the basis of the discussion which focused on the importance of planning and structure, carefully balanced by flexibility and opportunity. There was then a detailed consideration of how the teacher might provide an appropriate climate for learning central to which was the teacher-pupil relationship. Within this context there were suggestions regarding the organization and provision of a stimulating environment and appropriate materials and resources.

An outline of a framework for learning was exemplified through the detailed analysis of specific starting points for extended work with children and the way in which each starting point led to differing outcomes. This chapter was concluded by looking at the role of assessment in the edu-cational process.

One premise upon which this approach to learning is based is that sig-nificant learning requires appropriate and adequate time for working. A description of the rhythm of the school provided a different perspective through which to view the processes and practices of the school, class and individual child. As well as the day-to-day ebb and flow of school life, we aconsidered the longer-term effects of the school year and the points of tran-sition from one school to another. While acknowledging the various exter-nal constraints, we emphasized the ways in which the participants within the educational process can still affect the quality and nature of learning through the constructive use of time.

Nurturing the Organic Curriculum

Having described the antecedents and practices relating to the organic curriculum, the final section of the book addressed the issue of how organic teaching might be developed. The emphasis in this section was on the teacher and teacher development rather than the child. This was examined from two different but complementary standpoints.

Based upon the earlier descriptions of the organic curriculum in practice, we presented and illustrated an evolutionary model of how the teacher might develop a mode of operating which encompasses child-centred, integrated, process-oriented, active learning. The different stages of development were acknowledged and their relationship to actual activities was exemplified.

A major strand of our thesis is that for teachers to achieve satisfaction in the task of teaching through enabling and encouraging dynamic learning, they must take professional responsibility for their actions. In particular there is a need to be reflective, self-critical and self-developmental. However to achieve such ideals, an external priming of the pump may be necessary. The penultimate chapter addressed this by examining ways in which a school can facilitate staff development at an individual and a group level.

Reflections

Any statement of an approach to teaching runs the risk of focusing only on surface qualities and perhaps missing important underlying dimensions. We might use the analogy of topsoil in a garden which can nuture growth to a certain extent, but for sustained growth it needs a rich base from which to draw. Otherwise the topsoil must be repeatedly replaced. The organic curriculum presumes that techniques which operate only on the surface are transitory and that the development of enduring good practice requires a fundamental grounding in solid reflection and the building of a sound rationale. There is also the lesson to be gained from recognizing that the obvious qualities, while necessary, are certainly not sufficient in themselves.

Teachers have traditionally been seen as practitioners in the art of education. They have been encouraged to develop the skills of teaching through concentration on what shall be taught and how to teach it. The various pressures exerted on, for example, initial teacher training courses, the working school, and in service courses have allowed little time for reflection. They have often been concerned with the immediate needs of the participants. The outcome of such an approach is to improve individual practices without creating an underpinning theory of why such practices should occur and whether they are internally consistent. The amount of time taken in treating each incident, each curriculum area, each organizational issue as a here-and-now problem to be solved has meant that often there is no opportunity to discuss the reasons behind the actions.

If instead we can begin with the question 'why?', then the questions of 'how?' and 'what?' may follow more easily. Not only may they follow but they will be informed by an overarching philosophy which eases the decision making, creates a consistency and improves the learning processes for children and teachers alike. Throughout this book we have been more concerned with delineating practice as suggested and supported by theory rather than explicating fully all the questions raised by such practice.

A symptom of the concentration on practicalities to the neglect of a clear analysis and rationale is the simplistic nature of some of the statements made about classroom practices. The use of simple stereotypes is illustrated by a common practice of equating classroom organization with teaching style. If a classroom is organized in rows, it is assumed that the teaching style associated with it is didactic and 'closed', always centred on the teacher. On the other hand, if a teacher organizes the children so that they are sitting and working in groups, it is often assumed that the teaching style is open and exploratory.

In the first room, the children may be sitting in rows and working individually but the source of their inspiration, the nature of their learning experience may be far removed from that. They may have been involved in an experience based activity which involved not only handling materials but also cooperating with each other. Having done that, then they were writing about their work with individual concentration and endeavour.

In the second room the children were indeed sitting at tables and working in groups. One group was doing mathematics, another writing and a third one working with paint. On the face of it this is sometimes labelled 'integrated work' with children busily going about their business. However this pattern is maintained every day and all day and at the end of a working session the children move as on a merry-go-round to the next activity. This movement is dictated by the clock and the teacher. It is seldom if ever negotiable. A closer look at the activities shows that the mathematics group is working on the same page in the same mathematics book. Tomorrow they will go on to the next page. While they are engaged with this task the teacher is instructing the painters how to paint and what to paint. The writers are copying the teacher's writing from the blackboard. The children are working as isolated individuals sitting in groups.

These situations are not apocryphal. Neither are they exaggerated. They are descriptions of a reality. There are two important points to be made in reference to these descriptions. Firstly, teachers have to reflect on the needs of the children at a given time. In the light of that reflection teachers choose an appropriate organization and an appropriate style to achieve the intended goals. Secondly, if such reflection is to occur, teachers have to refine and develop the ability to observe, in particular the ability to observe the way in which children learn and work.

From such careful observation teachers gather relevant information in order to offer interpretations of what they see. They hypothesize as to possible causes of or hindrances to learning and the possible effects of their future actions. Decisions are made as to what might be appropriate interventions in the learning process. Teachers predict what might happen and then put their plans into action. As they observe the results of their actions the whole process begins again; observation, data collection, hypothesis, intervention, prediction.

It is a pattern which will be recognized by children attempting primary science as well as by researchers. If it were to be applied regularly to the classroom context it would not only sharpen awareness but also inform developments in practice. To some this plan may appear too simple and may be dismissed as an irrelevance, as something which thinking teachers do already with regard to both the children's learning and their own professional development. However the argument is that all teachers should be thinking teachers and all teachers should apply such rigour regularly and reflectively. The simplistic nature of the suggestion belies the difficulty of maintaining a high level of critical observation and reflective and informed action. However the results of such a process will lead to improved teacher-child interactions and classroom organization and a truly balanced and relevant curriculum.

The major emphasis of this book is about giving appropriate models and frameworks, a variety of paradigms, to be used by teachers to develop for themselves. In examining the various concepts and ideas, it is for teachers to decide what meaning such ideas have for them. As they reflect on the various frameworks of organization and models of teaching and learning, then teachers will consider whether such models have relevance to their situations. It is impossible and would, indeed, be inadvisable to attempt to operationalize every concept relevant to the organic curriculum. Depending on the individual perspective of each teacher, some of this range of suggestions will have immediate relevance. Other ideas will seem inappropriate. It is the teacher's responsibility to decide. There is no blueprint, no right or wrong, no master plan; but there is informed and reflective good practice.

A main thrust of our argument has been that teachers in the classroom still have influence. There has been an attempt to identify how power and control are available to teachers to determine pedagogy, conditions for learning and the curriculum. This empowerment is not concerned with the macro-issues of political and economic control but with the professional arena of the classroom.

In the preface we referred to the central role of the teacher as being to professionally examine the various options available in terms of learning experiences and teaching styles in order to achieve the results which society desires for its young. Schools and teachers have always operated within social and political parameters. There are clear expectations for the school. The nature of these expectations determines the amount of control the head and staff have over curriculum content and pedagogy. The detailed, centralized curriculum imposed at district or national levels denies the individuality of the learning process and the art of the professional teacher. In some cases such centralized curriculum may be designed by administrators or theoreticians with teachers acting only to implement a sterile checklist of activities and tests. As teachers in different settings assess the extent of the support they may receive in developing their practice, they may rightly perceive they have much help from colleagues and so function as part of a broader school-wide effort. Alternatively, in other circumstances, they may be operating virtually on their own. However centrally stated requirements do not comprise the totality of what can occur in the classroom. Whatever the constraints, whatever the climate, there is still some opportunity to exercise professional judgment.

Financial, cultural, political, historical and organizational parameters *are* powerful but wherever the teacher is, in terms of position in the system, geographical location or socio-economic setting, there is still *some* control over decision-making. No matter what constraints have to be faced, the responsibility for the learning and development of the children still rests upon the teacher. That is both the excitement and the difficulty of the teacher's task.

The way in which such learning and development might be achieved is very much within the professional arena. We assert that it is for the teacher to consider whether the child is to be at the centre of the learning process. Child-centred learning is not to be misinterpreted as letting children do whatever they wish to do. It is for the teacher to consider the efficacy and appropriateness of experience-based, process-oriented learning. And it is for the teacher to assess the totality of the learning experience and the degree to which areas of experience and knowledge can be isolated or integrated. If careful consideration has been given to those elements of the curriculum then, whatever the teacher's decisions, he or she will be better equipped to argue in support of their professional actions.

The future is always unknown. It is possible that we are now in a time when we know more about how best to help children learn than we have ever known. We will need to employ this knowledge with skill and sensitivity if we are to meet the demands of a new technological age. The future of our children continues to lie heavily in the hands of the classroom teacher. The decisions which are necessary to fulfil the potential of the children in our care cannot be abrogated.

References

ADAMS, A. and REYNOLDS, S. (1981) 'The long conversation: Tracing the roots of the past', in *Journal of Experiential Education*, 4, 1, pp. 21–8.

ALEXANDER, R.J. (1984) *Primary Teaching*, London, Holt, Rinehart and Winston.

BARNES, D. (1982) *Practical Curriculum Study*, London, Routledge and Kegan Paul.

BARTH, R.S. (1972) 'Open education: Assumptions about children, learning, and knowledge', in PURPEL, D.E. and BELANGER, M. (Eds.) *Curriculum and the Cultural Revolution*, Berkeley, California, McCutchan, pp. 424–54.

BENNETT, N. *et al.* (1980) 'Open plan primary schools: Findings and implications of a national inquiry', in *Education 3–13*, 8, 1, pp. 45–50.

BERMAN, L.M. (1968) *New Priorities in the Curriculum*, Columbus, Ohio, Charles E. Merrill.

BLACKIE, J. (1967) *Inside the Primary School*, New York, Schocken Books.

BLACKIE, J. (1974) *Transforming the Primary School*, New York, Schocken Books.

BLENKIN, G.M. and KELLY, A.V. (1987) *The Primary Curriculum: A Process Approach to Curriculum Planning*, 2nd ed., London, Harper and Row.

BLYTH, W.A.L. (1965) *English Primary Education: A Sociological Description* (Vols. 1 and 2), London, Routledge and Kegan Paul.

BLYTH, W.A.L. (1984) *Development, Experience and Curriculum in Primary Education*, London, Croom Helm.

BONNETT, M. (1986) 'Child-centredness, and the problem of structure in project work', in *Cambridge Journal of Education*, 16, 1, pp. 3–6.

BRADLEY, H. (1983) 'Developing pupils' thinking through topic work', in *Primary Education Review*, 18, pp. 11–13.

BRANDT, R.M. (1975) 'An observational portrait of a British infant school', in SPODEK, B. and WALBERG, H.J. (Eds.) *Studies in Open Education*, New York, Agathon Press, pp. 101–25.

BRENNAN, A. (1985) 'Primary education in the eighties', in *British Journal of Educational Studies*, 33, 3, pp. 278–99.

BROWN, M. and PRECIOUS, N. (1968) *The Integrated Day in the Primary School*, London, Ward Lock.

BRUNER, J.S. (1960) *The Process of Education*, New York, Random House.

BUTT, R.L. (1977) *The Development of a Conceptual System for the Open Classroom*, Unpublished doctoral dissertation, University of Ottawa.

CANGELOSI, J.S. (1988) *Classroom Management Strategies: Gaining and Maintaining*

Students' Cooperation, New York, Longman.

CENTRAL ADVISORY COUNCIL FOR EDUCATION (1967) *Children and Their Primary Schools* (Vols. 1 and 2) (The Plowden Report), London, HMSO.

CLEGG, A.B. (1971) *Revolution in the British Primary Schools*, Washington, DC, National Association of Elementary School Principals.

CLEGG, A.B. (1972) 'Closing talk', West Riding Vacation Course, Unpublished manuscript, Yorkshire.

CLOUGH, E.E., BAILEY, A., BOWLEY, R. and COLDRON, J. (1985) 'Can topic work be assessed?', in *Education 3–13*, 13, 1, pp. 37–44.

CONNER, C. (1986) 'Children's learning and project work', in *Cambridge Journal of Education*, 16, 1, pp. 11–16.

CREMIN, L.A. (1961) *The Transformation of the School: Progressivism in American Education, 1876–1957*, New York, Alfred A. Knopf.

DALE, E. (1969) *Audiovisual Methods in Teaching*, 3rd ed., New York, Holt, Rinehart and Winston.

DARLING, J. (1986) 'Child-centred, gender-centred: A criticism of progressive curriculum theory from Rousseau to Plowden', in *Oxford Review of Education*, 12, 1, pp. 31–40.

DEARDEN, R.F. (1976) *Problems in Primary Education*, London, Routledge and Kegan Paul.

DEPARTMENT OF EDUCATION AND SCIENCE (1949) *Story of a School — Education Pamphlet 14*, London, HMSO.

DEPARTMENT OF EDUCATION AND SCIENCE (1975) *A Language for Life* (The Bullock Report), London, HMSO.

DEPARTMENT OF EDUCATION AND SCIENCE (1978) *Primary Education in England: A Survey by HM Inspectors of Schools*, London, HMSO.

DEPARTMENT OF EDUCATION AND SCIENCE (1980) *A View of the Curriculum: HMI Series: Matters for Discussion No. 11*, London, HMSO.

DEPARTMENT OF EDUCATION AND SCIENCE (1982a) *Education 5–9: An Illustrative Survey of 80 First Schools in England*, London, HMSO.

DEPARTMENT OF EDUCATION AND SCIENCE (1982b) *Mathematics Counts* (The Cockcroft Report), London, HMSO.

DEPARTMENT OF EDUCATION AND SCIENCE (1983) *9–13 Middle Schools: An Illustrative Survey*, London, HMSO.

DEPARTMENT OF EDUCATION AND SCIENCE (1985a) *The Curriculum from 5 to 16: Curriculum Matters 2: An HMI Series*, London, HMSO.

DEPARTMENT OF EDUCATION AND SCIENCE (1985b) *Education 8 to 12 in Combined and Middle Schools*, London, HMSO.

DEPARTMENT OF EDUCATION AND SCIENCE (1985c) *Better Schools* (White Paper), London, HMSO.

DEPARTMENT OF EDUCATION AND SCIENCE (1986) *English from 5 to 16:·The Responses to Curriculum Matters 1: An HMI Report*, London, HMSO.

DEWEY, J. (1902) *The Child and the Curriculum*, Chicago, University of Chicago Press.

DEWEY, J. (1916) *Democracy and Education*, New York, Macmillan.

DEWEY, J. (1931) *The Way Out of Educational Confusion*, Westport, Connecticut, Greenwood Press.

DEWEY, J. (1938) *Experience and Education*, New York, Macmillan.

DOLL, W.E. (1983) 'A re-visioning of progressive education', in *Theory Into Practice*, 22, 3, pp. 166–73.

EASTHOPE, G. (1975) *Community, Hierarchy and Open Education*, London, Routledge and Kegan Paul.

EGGLESTON, J. (1984) 'What did the children learn?', in *Education 3–13*, 12, 1, pp. 28–32.

EISNER, E.W. (1973) *English Primary Schools: Some Observations and Assessments*, Palo Alto, California, Stanford University.

EISNER, E.W. (1982) *Cognition and Curriculum: A Basis for Deciding What to Teach*, New York, Longman.

ELLSWORTH, R. (1979) 'Research on open education: Do we need a moratorium?', in *Education*, 100, 2, pp. 149–52.

ENTWISTLE, H. (1970) *Child-Centred Education*, London, Methuen.

EVANS, J.T. (1975) 'An activity analysis of US traditional, US open, and British open classrooms', in SPODEK, B. and WALBERG, H.J. (Eds.) *Studies in Open Education*, New York, Agathon Press, pp. 155–68.

FEATHERSTONE, J. (1971) *Schools Where Children Learn*, New York, Liveright.

FISHER, R.J. (1972) *Learning How to Learn: The English Primary School and American Education*, New York, Harcourt Brace Jovanovich.

FUNK, H.J., FIEL, R.L., OKEY, J.R., JAUS, H.H. and SPRAGUE, C.S. (1985) *Learning Science Process Skills*, 2nd ed., Dubuque, Iowa, Kendall/Hunt.

GALTON, M. and SIMON, B. (Eds.) (1980) *Progress and Performance in the Primary Classroom*, London, Routledge and Kegan Paul.

GALTON, M., SIMON, B. and CROLL, P. (1980) *Inside the Primary Classroom*, London, Routledge and Kegan Paul.

GALTON, M. and WILLCOCKS, J. (Eds.) (1983) *Moving from the Primary Classroom*, London, Routledge and Kegan Paul.

GIACONIA, R.M. and HEDGES, L.V. (1982) 'Identifying features of effective open education', in *Review of Educational Research*, 52, 4, pp. 579–602.

GLASSER, W. (1986) *Control Theory in the Classroom*, New York, Harper and Row.

GOOD, T.L. and BROPHY, J.E. (1984) *Looking in Classrooms*, 3rd ed., New York, Harper and Row.

GRAY, J. and SATTERLY, D. (1981) 'Formal or informal? A re-assessment of the British evidence', in *British Journal of Educational Psychology*, 51, 2, pp. 187–96.

GRIFFIN-BEALE, C. (1975) 'Less of a gardener, more of a bee', in *The Times Educational Supplement*, 19 September, p. 23.

HAWKINS, D. (1973) 'The triangular relationship of teacher, student, and materials', in SILBERMAN, C.E. (Ed.) *The Open Classroom Reader*, New York, Random House, pp. 364–73.

HORWITZ, R.A. (1979) 'Psychological effects of the "open classroom"', in *Review of Educational Research*, 49, 1, pp. 71–85.

ISHLER, M.F. and ISHLER, R.E. (1974) 'Instructional skills of the British primary teacher and their implications for teacher education', in *Winds of Change: Teacher Education for the Open Area School*, Washington, DC, Association of Teacher Educators, pp. 11–18.

JOPLIN, L. (1981) 'On defining experiential education', in *Journal of Experiential Education*, 4, 1, pp. 17–20.

KELLY, A.V. (1986) *Knowledge and Curriculum Planning*, London, Harper and Row.

KERRY, T. (1983) 'Developing pupils' thinking through topic work', in *Education 3–13*, 11, 2, pp. 4–7.

KERRY, T. (1984 a) 'Effective training for topic teaching', in *Education 3–13*, 12, 1, pp. 33–7.

KERRY, T. (1984 b) 'Trialling in-service materials for topic work teaching', in *Cambridge Journal of Education*, 14, 1, pp. 25–30.

KILPATRICK, W.H. (1918) *The Project Method: The Use of the Purposeful Act in the Educative Process*, New York, Teachers College, Columbia University.

KOHL, H.R. (1969) *The Open Classroom*, New York, Random House.

LAWTON, D. (1975) *Class, Culture and the Curriculum*, London, Routledge and Kegan Paul.

LEITH, S. (1981) 'Project work: An enigma', in SIMON, B. and WILLCOCKS, J. (Eds.) *Research and Practice in the Primary Classroom*, London, Routledge and Kegan Paul, pp. 55–64.

MARRIOTT, S. (1985) *Primary Education and Society*, Lewes, Falmer Press.

MARSH, L. (1970) *Alongside the Child in the Primary School*, London, A. and C. Black.

MARSHALL, H.H. (1981) 'Open classrooms: Has the term outlived its usefulness?', in *Review of Educational Research*, 51, 2, pp. 181–92.

MARSHALL, S. (1963) *An Experiment in Education*, London, Cambridge University Press.

MILES, A. (1984) 'A closer look: A case study of topic work in the classroom', in *Education 3–13*, 12, 1, pp. 22–7.

MORGAN, L., *et al.* (1981) *Beyond the Open Classroom: Toward Informal Education*, Palo Alto, California, R and E Research Associates.

MYERS, D.A. and DUKE, D.L. (1977) 'Open education as an ideology', in *Educational Research*, 19, 3, pp. 227–35.

NODDINGS, N. and ENRIGHT, D.S. (1983) 'The promise of open education', in *Theory Into Practice*, 22, 3, pp. 182–9.

O'BRIEN, T.C. (1974) 'Some comments on British education', in *The Elementary School Journal*, 75, 1, pp. 42–9.

PHENIX, P.H. (1964) *Realms of Meaning*, New York, McGraw-Hill.

PIRSIG, R.M. (1976) *Zen and the Art of Motorcycle Maintenance*, London, Transworld.

POLLARD, A. (1985) *The Social World of the Primary School*, London, Holt, Rinehart and Winston.

POLLARD, A. (1987) 'Introduction: New perspectives on children', in POLLARD, A. (Ed.) *Children and Their Primary Schools: A New Perspective*, Lewes, Falmer Press, pp. 1–11.

PRATT, D. (1987) 'Curriculum design as humanistic technology', in *Journal of Curriculum Studies*, 19, 2, pp. 149–62.

PRING, R.A. (1970) 'Curriculum integration', in *Bulletin, University of London Institute of Education*, New Series Number 20, pp. 4–8.

PRING, R.A. (1976) *Knowledge and Schooling*, Wells, Somerset, Open Books.

RATHBONE, C.H. (Ed.) (1971) *Open Education: The Informal Classroom*, New York, Citation Press.

RAZZELL, A. (1968) *Juniors: A Postscript to Plowden*, Harmondsworth, Middlesex, Penguin.

RESNICK, L.B. (1972) 'Teacher behavior in an informal British infant school', in *School Review*, 81, 1, pp. 63–83.

RICHARDS, C. (1980) 'Demythologizing primary education', in *Journal of Curriculum Studies*, 12, 1, pp. 77–8.

RICHARDS, C. (1982) 'Primary education: 1974–80', in RICHARDS, C. (Ed.) *New Directions in Primary Education*, Lewes, Falmer Press, pp. 7–22.

RICHARDS, C. (1984) *The Study of Primary Education: A Source Book, Volume 1*, Lewes, Falmer Press.

ROGERS, V.R. (1970) *Teaching in the British Primary School*, London, Collier-Macmillan.

ROWLAND, S. (1984) *The Enquiring Classroom: An Approach to Understanding Children's Learning*, Lewes, Falmer Press.

SCHILLER, C. (1979) *Christian Schiller: In His Own Words*, London, A. and C. Black.

SCHOOLS COUNCIL (1983) *Schools Council Working Paper 75 — Primary Practice: A Sequel to 'The Practical Curriculum'*, London, Methuen.

SCHWAB, J.J. (1962) 'The concept of the structure of a discipline', in *Educational Record*, 43, 3, pp. 197–205.

SHARP, R. and GREEN, A. (1975) *Education and Social Control: A Study in Progressive Primary Education*, London, Routledge and Kegan Paul.

SILBERMAN, C.E. (1970) *Crisis in the Classroom: The Remaking of American Education*, New York, Random House.

STEPHENS, L.S. (1974) *The Teacher's Guide to Open Education*, New York, Holt, Rinehart and Winston.

STEWART, W.A.C. (1979) 'Progressive education: Past, present and future', in *British Journal of Educational Studies*, 27, 2, pp. 103–10.

TANNER, R. (1981) *The Way We Have Come — Children as Artists and Craftsmen 1907–81*, Unpublished manuscript, Woolley Hall College, West Yorkshire.

THOMAS, S.C. and WALBERG, H.J. (1975) 'An analytic review of the literature', in SPODEK, B. and WALBERG, H.J. (Eds.) *Studies in Open Education*, New York, Agathon Press, pp. 13–41.

WATERS, D. (1982) *Primary School Projects*, London, Heinemann.

WEBB, N. (1986) 'Structure and child participation in project work: One school's response', in *Cambridge Journal of Education*, 16, 1, pp. 6–11.

WEBER, L. (1971) *The English Infant School and Informal Education*, Englewood Cliffs, New Jersey, Prentice-Hall.

WHITE, J.J. (1986) 'Decision-making with an integrative curriculum', in *Childhood Education*, 62, 5, pp. 337–43.

WHITEHEAD, A.N. (1929) *The Aims of Education and Other Essays*, New York, Macmillan.

WRAY, D. (1985) *Teaching Information Skills through Project Work*, London, Hodder and Stoughton.

Index